SOUVENIRS FROM AN

ABSURD LIFE

A MEMOIR

DON DAHLER

Post Hill
PRESS

A POST HILL PRESS BOOK
ISBN: 979-8-88845-857-0
ISBN (eBook): 979-8-88845-858-7

Souvenirs from an Absurd Life:
A Memoir
© 2025 by Don Dahler
All Rights Reserved

Cover design by Cody Corcoran
Cover photo by Daniel Leocadi

Post Hill Press
New York • Nashville
posthillpress.com

Published in the United States of America
1 2 3 4 5 6 7 8 9 10

CONTENTS

A MOST UNLIKELY PATH

For a while, I was that guy. Nice suit. Tasteful tie. Not a hair out of place. An anchorman in the nation's largest television market, earnestly talking to viewers about the terrible things people do to each other, or how the financial markets are affecting their retirement plans, or how bad the coming storm will be, as I toss in a quip to the friendly neighborhood weatherman.

And for a while I was also that other guy you see on television: the one reporting from all over the country and the world about the bigger picture, the criminal trials, the crippling floods, the endless wars, as a correspondent for Fox News, CNBC, ABC News, and, lastly, CBS News.

"Correspondent," by the way, is just a fancy name for television reporters who've made it to the national stage. Kind of how a chef is really just a talented cook whose name is now on the menu. There are plenty of people working for your local news who are better reporters than many network correspondents, myself included. Those journalists either prefer working in local news, don't have as good an agent, or simply don't have the desired look, regional accent, or alma mater. Being elevated to the rarified air of a news network is about as subjective a process as can be. Think *Jeopardy!* meets the *Miss America* pageant meets *The Hunger Games*: push the button at the right moment, have all the correct answers, and look exactly like who the executives have in mind while also managing to survive the unbelievably cutthroat competition. For a television journalist, it's the equivalent of hitting the career Powerball lottery. But there are strings attached. So many strings.

The fact that I was among those very few elevated to that position, for as long as I was able to hang on to it, is absolutely ridiculous.

I ran away from an abusive father while still in high school. By working as a busboy, waiter, auto mechanic, and country-western DJ—one who bluffed his way into the job without knowing dick about country music—I managed to scrape together enough money each month to pay rent and car expenses. I lived on restaurant leftovers and cheese sandwiches. My prospects were grim. Often the thought "Is this all there is?" crept into my mind, and I knew I couldn't bear such a future.

College was out of the question, since, as an independent but not legally emancipated minor, I didn't qualify for any loans or grants based on my father's income. The $1,600 my mom once put away into Treasury bills for my education went toward fixing my car when an errant drainpipe in the middle of the road ripped out the transmission. And that was pretty much how I saw my life going at that point—survive, pay the bills, and hope for a break, any break. I had no earthly idea what form that break could take.

One afternoon while I was bartending at a popular club in Dallas, a man sat down at the end of the bar, someone instantly recognizable to anyone who followed sports back then: Dick Enberg, the most eloquent and authentically warm announcer to ever sit before a microphone.

He was in town for a Cowboys game and had time to kill. We chatted amiably in the almost-empty bar. He told me about his career and his life on the road; what he loved about it; who his favorite athletes were…

At some point, he turned to me and asked how old I was.
"Twenty-one," I said.

"So what are you doing here, then?"

I laughed and deflected. "Just getting by. You know…"

"Is that what you want to do? Just get by?"

I don't remember having a good answer to that. I think I told him about loving writing and photography and about helping to start a school newspaper in junior high. He asked if I liked journalism. I'm relatively certain I responded yes. I especially liked the freedom of it. I learned early on that being on the staff of a school newspaper gave me the golden ticket—a hall pass—that got me out of almost any class to photograph very important events, such as cheerleading practice.

"Maybe you should look into that as a career," he suggested.

I had no idea how to even begin. And I told him that.

"Well, what most people do is go to college, get an internship at a local station, and absorb everything they can about how television news works. You're young. It might take a while, but if you really want it and work really hard, I think you'll make it."

This conversation was a transformative moment for me. I moved back to San Antonio, enrolled in the local community college, and eventually landed unpaid internships at KSAT-TV and then KENS. These internships directly lead to my first job in television. I'd found my true love: combining storytelling, photography, and a never-ending source of learning.

By the way, I still have the autographed photo Mr. Enberg sent me years later after I wrote a letter thanking him for changing my life. It bears his famous catchphrase: "Oh my!" That generous man had spent the better part of an hour acting as the guidance counselor I never had, helping me see what was really possible. But what he also did was put me back in touch with a promise I'd made over a decade earlier.

I was nine years old, getting ready for bed in my family's Colorado Springs home. I hit my knees and started my nightly prayers. My family wasn't overly religious, but it was a comforting ritual to give thanks for the good things and make a few requests, just in case someone up there was listening. I'd always ask for God to bless my best friends Ray and Dana—the twin girls who lived across the street until they were killed in a horrific car accident—and to keep Dad safe if and when he was sent to Vietnam, that far-off, confusing war being waged on our television set every night at dinnertime.

But that evening I had a very specific request. I remember it clearly. I made a deal with God. I didn't care about being rich or famous, I told him. I wanted to live an adventurous life like those led by my favorite characters in all the books and TV shows I devoured: Huckleberry Finn. E.C. Gordon. Jonny Quest. Meg Murry.

The idea of living a boring life working a miserable nine-to-five job filled me with despair. So, in return, I promised God that if he set me on a path filled with exciting experiences, I'd be a good person. Seemed a fair trade-off.

That deal provided a map to the realization of the dream Dick Enberg laid out before me years later at that Dallas bar.

This book is a collection of moments—souvenirs, if you will—of my journey from military brat to run away to local television reporter to documentary filmmaker to network correspondent. I've been shot and shot at more times than I care to remember. I've seen more war and death up close than anyone ever should. I was bitten by a shark and briefly held the American record for diving 150 feet underwater on a single breath of air, both on live TV. I've interviewed Nobel Prize recipients, future presidents, Olympic champions, and countless movie stars. I've had lions stalk outside my tent in Africa, tracked a fox through miles of desert, tamed a wild fruit bat, and flown in an ultralight airplane over the heads of elephants. I've walked through central Asian mountain passes where no Westerner had stood for hundreds of years. And I was an eyewitness to one of the worst days in our nation's history.

The following stories are true. I've tried to tell them as accurately as possible to the best of my memory and using journals I've kept most of my life. There are some key names I've regretfully forgotten, and I apologize to anyone I've left out of these accounts, some of whom will no doubt be relieved. I still have no idea how it all happened, how I've been so fortunate as to have this life and all these different, fascinating careers. Some talent. Hard work, for sure. Good timing. Luck played more than a small part. And, yes, that prayer by a little boy kneeling beside his bed was definitely answered, whether by a benevolent deity or by simple fate. Whatever the mysterious alchemy that made it possible, I'm forever grateful.

These stories are loosely chronological. In no way are they intended to be a how-to guide for aspiring journalists and authors—other than, perhaps, in demonstrating the one philosophy that has proven to be true again and again.

If you want it, you have to go get it.

CHAPTER 1

HOW TO GET SHOT—TWICE

Pretty much every Christmas since I was, oh, a zygote, I'd ask Santa for a horse. And pretty much every Christmas morning I'd look outside and see—trees and leaves and grass and no horse. This went on for years. Every Christmas the same thing. The same disappointment. The same completely valid excuse by my parents: We're a military family. We move all the time. We can't own a horse.

When I was ten, we were living in Klamath Falls, Oregon, at an Air Force base named Kingsley Field. It was summertime. Our base housing area butted up to some vacant hills and farmland. I'd wander around for hours, building rock-and-wood forts or looking to scrape out a tree house like the guy in *My Side of the Mountain*, one of my favorite books at the time. Unfortunately, there were no trees large enough, and certainly no trees partially burned by a lightning strike, to afford such accommodations.

One day while wandering the hills I spotted a pasture with a small, brown pony munching on his lunch. As I walked up to the wire fence, he lifted his head and started trotting over to me. He was friendly and curious, and probably a little lonely. On a sudden impulse I ducked through the fence, hefted myself onto his back, and started riding him around the pasture. Slowly at first, then faster, hanging on with nothing but a good grip on his mane. It was heaven. He seemed to enjoy it too. (Although knowing what I know now about this marvelous species, he was likely just enjoying the company. Horses are wonderfully social creatures.)

Every chance I got, I would sneak over to that farm with an apple or carrot or bag of Lay's potato chips, whatever I could steal from home. The pony was always waiting at the fence for me. He'd gleefully chomp on whatever treat I'd brought, then stand perfectly still as I wiggled and squirmed to get onto his back. We'd ride for an hour or so, I'd slide off his sweaty back, we'd say our goodbyes, and I'd head home, sore-butted and happy as could be.

First day of school came. My big sister, Meg, and I walked to our new elementary school. Meg was a grade ahead of me.

I'm going to sound like the boomer I am for a second because I don't know how else to explain this. Schools today have all kinds of rules about bullies and violence and "don't put your hands on Bobby." But back then, when a military brat moved into town, there was always some numbskull at every school who had to challenge the new kid to a fight. Sometimes more than one kid. It was a Darwinian effort to establish the pecking order. I hated it. But after a few moves from town to town, I realized you either learn how to fight or learn how to cower.

So that day, there was a guy, slightly larger than me, who asked a lot of questions at lunch about where I was from, who my dad was, what sports I liked, and so on. For a foolish second, I thought, Hey, I may have stumbled on a great friend! When the school day finished, he found me at the entrance, put his arm around my shoulder, and said, "Hey, come on, let me show you around." We started walking.

Then I saw it. They were all waiting. All the kids in our grade. The word had spread through the whisper network. They stood in a circle in a vacant lot just off school grounds and turned to watch us approach. My sister was walking a few steps behind. I couldn't see her face. I'm sure she had no idea what to do.

He suddenly pushed me into the center of the circle and said, "We're going to fight." I'm not kidding. That's exactly what he said. I can hear his voice to this day.

"I don't want to fight you," I said, looking for a gap in the crowd.

"You're going to." He took a wild swing. I grabbed him awkwardly and wrestled him to the ground.

"I'm not going to fight you!"

"Yes you are!"

We tussled around in the dirt for a few minutes before he pulled free, and we stood again. He took another swing and missed.

"Just stop it!" I yelled. "We don't have to do this!"

"Yes we do!"

So I hit him. Hard. Directly on the nose. One of the only things I'd ever learned from my dad is how to throw a punch. Unfortunately, I was always on the receiving end of his. Until the very last one. Maybe I'll tell you about that later.

Back to the vacant lot. When my punch connected, I saw blood spurt out from either side of my fist. The boy's eyes went wide. He went down. The crowd cheered. Not for me, of course. Just for the violence.

He stayed down, holding both hands to his face. I felt someone pulling at my arms. Meg was telling me it was time to leave.

We walked in silence back to the house.

As we neared the front door, our dad threw it open and bellowed for me to get inside. Mom stood in a corner of the living room. I couldn't read her expression, but there was some mix of fear or concern sprinkled in it. I'm pretty sure Mom was more afraid of our father than any of us were. She lived with that human volcano a lot longer than we did.

"What the hell are you trying to do? Get us sued?" Dad shouted. His face was crimson. His eyes were bloodshot. His fists were clinched at his sides as if he was trying to strangle the life out of two little sparrows. "This boy's father just called me and said you broke his nose! Do you have any idea what that means? We could go to court! They could take everything we own! I'm an officer, for God's sake! This could cost me a promotion!"

This from the man who, after I came home from getting beaten up the first time, coached me that when facing the prospect of a fight, hit first, and hit hard.

"He started it," I said meekly, trying not to cry. "I didn't want to fight."

Meg nodded.

Dad's face was now purple. "That doesn't matter. You better hope they don't sue us. You better hope!"

Ah, the inconsistencies of life.

He stormed away. I don't think he hit me before he left the room, but my memory is a little foggy. And I was used to that by then.

The good news is that nobody messed with me at school anymore. That particular school, I mean. I got in fights pretty much every year until the end of high school.

Not too long afterward, I was riding the little pony again when I heard a shout. I turned to see a man running across the pasture with what looked like a shotgun in his hands. He seemed angry.

I jumped off the horse and began dashing toward the fence, but the ground was muddy and uneven. I couldn't get a good footing.

I felt it before I heard it. My back lit up like fire in a hundred places, and then I heard a large pop. I stumbled to one knee, got up, and kept running. The man kept shouting. But I didn't hear another gunshot. I made it to the fence, dove between the wire strands, and ran all the way home. I never went back to see the horse.

I also never told my parents. I could imagine my dad being enraged about the possibility of being sued. I threw away the tattered, bloodied shirt. How long does it take to die from a gunshot? I remember wondering.

I'm lucky. Turns out the farmer had loaded his shotgun with salt, not pellets. For years I had little blue dots on my back. They finally faded away when I was about twenty. I do realize the horse's owner was well within his rights. I was trespassing on his land. A ten-year-old boy who only wanted to ride a lonely pony. But, yeah, stand your ground and all that. Good on you.

In the ensuing decades I've been shot at by numerous people in war zones all over the world, the rounds sometimes passing close enough that I could see the tracers zip by in front of my face. Fortunately, all those guys missed. That autumn day in Oregon I was shot by my own countryman. The first time, obviously. But not the last.

Los Angeles. August 14, 2000. The Democratic National Convention. I was covering the demonstrations outside the Staples Center, where Al Gore and Joe Lieberman were being nominated as the Democrats' presidential ticket. A few days earlier, a court had ordered the city to move the designated "protest zone" from a block away from the arena to an open space adjacent to it. The LAPD, after having just tussled with rioters a month earlier when celebrations over the Lakers' winning the NBA championship turned violent, were in a sour mood. This was only a few years after the Rampart scandal broke, one in which seventy officers were implicated in crimes ranging from planted evidence to theft to murder. The LAPD was widely seen as corrupt and racist. And, boy, did its officers hate the news media for reporting on it.

The protests outside the convention were a hodgepodge of antiabortion supporters, anarchists, homeless activists, and anti-globalizationists. The rock band Rage Against the Machine, known for some antipolice lyrics, played in their midst, stoking much of the anger. Judging by the dark looks on the faces of the cops, they were not loving it.

Late in the evening, the dozens of journalists keeping an eye on things, including me and my colleagues from ABC News, noticed an increase in tensions between the cops and the almost ten thousand protesters. The LAPD was quoted in a Los Angeles Times article: "[S]everal people began throwing pieces of concrete, metal rods and glass bottles over a fence at police. Others started pulling up metal signs and setting bonfires."[1] I must have been looking at the stars or something. I never saw any of that. Nonetheless, mounted units were brought to the front, slowly closing in on the crowd of protesters at Olympic Boulevard and Figueroa Street.

As soon as the concert finished, a loudspeaker squawked, and an officer announced the protests were being disbanded. It was declared an illegal assembly. Eight thousand people were given fifteen minutes to leave. I can objectively state that I could never have gotten my two young kids out the door and into the car in that amount of time.

At that point, I did notice water bottles, curses, and sundry small items tossed in the direction of the huge phalanx of police dressed in riot gear, carrying ballistic shields, and wearing helmets with clear plastic face guards. The yelling increased.

Suddenly, the police began marching forward as a single unit. There was pushing and the wet thuds of batons thwacking backs and heads. Tear gas wafted in the air.

We journalists realized very quickly that we were trapped between the cops and the objects of their ire. It was not a great place to be. We were being aggressively herded out of the parking area along with the protesters, and there was no place

---

1   McGreevy, Patrick. "Lawsuit from in 2000 Settled." *Los Angeles Times.* May 4, 2004.

to duck out of the way. We loudly identified ourselves as news media. We waved press credentials. Didn't matter.

That's when we began hearing the shots and screams. Some of the police in the front rows were firing beanbags and rubber bullets. That's somewhat of a misnomer. These particular rubber bullets, nicknamed "skippers," are hard projectiles designed to be shot at the ground to fragment into painful but (normally) nonlethal shards that pepper legs and "encourage" protesters to keep moving. But it quickly became obvious that some of these cops were deliberately firing directly at civilians against department procedural rules. How do I know? Because they shot me and my cameraman. Point blank. From about ten feet away.

They got me twice. In the upper-middle back and lower right. I felt the bullets enter with the force of a sledgehammer. The only reason I didn't immediately collapse to the ground was because I was propelled into the mass of humanity I was already pushing up against. The large projectiles didn't tear into my body and shred organs like actual metal bullets—they both popped out like bowling balls dropped into a trampoline—but I still have the scars to this day. For weeks my back was an orange and black and red and purple and yellow panoply of pain. I had trouble taking deep breaths. Others were not as lucky. One woman named Melissa Schneider took a rubber bullet to the face. She's permanently blinded in one eye. Another journalist suffered nerve damage to his groin. A seventy-five-year-old man was almost crippled by a shot to his lower back. In all, the city of Los Angeles paid out over $4 million to settle a class-action lawsuit over the actions of the police. I wasn't part of that suit.

As they began disbursing the checks, city officials maintained that the Los Angeles Police Department did nothing wrong in its dealings with the demonstrations. The settlements were, according to an LAPD source quoted in the Los Angeles Times, "business decisions made to avoid the cost of full trials."[2] Nothing to see here, folks. Just the price of freedom. In an odd moment of saying the quiet part out loud, the LAPD also admitted there was no video evidence of "the violence committed by protesters against officers, so a jury might conclude that the officers used rubber bullets unnecessarily, thus violating constitutional rights." Yup. Including, oh, let's see, maybe a few journalists' First Amendment rights?

Don't bother Googling my report from that evening. It never made air. I was informed by a senior producer that the higher-ups didn't want to make the story "about us."

---

2   Ibid.

CHAPTER 2

ALLIGATORS AND IDIOTS

Her eyes were barely visible above the water, watching us with primordial, lethal calm. I nudged our narrow canoe, called a "pirogue" in those parts, a little closer to her as David, my friend and coconspirator, angled the rope tied to a smelly opossum carcass around the other side of the boat.

The gator began to advance. In long, sweeping movements, she glided closer to the bait. "Now!" David shouted.

I began to reverse course, and the gator followed. Five feet, ten feet, thirty feet away from her nest at the bank of one of the bayous that laced the area. She was following the rancid roadkill we'd scraped up from the highway. After a few days stewing in a trash bag at the far end of my grandparents' yard, the possum was at the height of its disgustingly smelly powers of attraction.

Whenever our dad went overseas, the rest of my family and I often moved in with Mom's parents, Jack and Verna Burns, in Baton Rouge. This particular time, Dad was in Vietnam. I must have been about eleven. David lived down the street on Riveroaks Drive, and we quickly became best friends for the summer. He was originally from Australia and loved adventure and the outdoors. We had a pact to run away Down Under together someday and buy a cattle ranch. "It's like the American Wild West," he told me more than once.

Gators aren't the most intelligent of creatures. Once the mama was lured far enough away so that we had enough time to raid the nest, David tied the rope to a tree limb, and we paddled as quickly as we could back to where the tiny six-inch-long babies were waiting. He scooped up a half dozen of the wiggly black reptiles, and we got out of there before the big female returned. Amazingly, none of the mamas ever chased us—even when they saw us near their nests. We deliberately left at least half of the young ones behind, hoping gators couldn't count. Worked every time.

Anyway, I can't remember which of us came up with the idea of catching and selling baby alligators to the area's pet stores, but after three such escapades we had already netted over sixty dollars. The stores paid five bucks a gator and sold them for a hundred. Eventually Baton Rouge passed a law making it illegal to own alligators as pets. More than likely, the babies we sold ended up back in the bayous once they got too big for their owners to handle.

Or, perhaps, the sewers of New York.

CHAPTER 3

THE DREAMERS OF THE DAY
ARE DANGEROUS MEN

I have no idea why I still have it, but I'm looking at the faded piece of paper now: a green and white dot-matrix computer printout. The title reads "General Aptitude Test Battery, Ohio Testing Services Division of Guidance and Testing." The next line lists my name and age, "15 years, 5 months"; "Grade 10"; "Test group 13."

Maybe I kept it all these years to reassure myself that sometimes the experts don't know crap. I have a box full of unpublished novels that I'd like to believe serve the same purpose but more likely demonstrate that the craft of writing takes a long, long time to perfect. Those old manuscripts are like ghost limbs for an amputee. Dead and useless, but somehow still attached to my soul.

Aptitude tests are no longer standard, as far as I know, but back then they were designed, presumably in good faith, to better guide students into the careers they were best cut out for. We sat in the library at Fairborn Baker High School near Dayton, Ohio, and answered a seemingly endless list of random questions. There were also manual dexterity tests, as I recall. I can picture the analysts going over the results: "Is he better at pushing buttons or turning a wrench?"

It was my junior year. My dad was temporarily stationed at Wright-Patterson Air Force Base and didn't want to be alone, so he dragged me along before the rest of the family eventually joined us, ripping me away from friends, sports, and my life in San Antonio. It wasn't all bad. The school was tiny, so I took part in pretty much every activity I could get into on and off school grounds: football, tennis, karate, boxing, and, of course, the school newspaper. I even acted in school plays. Because Dad was working really long days and traveling quite a bit, I was granted a hardship driver's license at fifteen. Mom loaned me her little red 1967 VW Beetle to tool around in. I still have it to this day.

Putting an unsupervised teen into his own car was a bit of a sketchy move in a state where many liquor stores were drive-throughs. I can't remember a single moment when the clerk at the window asked to see my driver's license. Genesee Cream Ale was my favorite, next to Boone's Farm Strawberry Hill wine. I should put "wine" in quotes—it was more like strawberry-flavored sugary alcohol. Needless to say, I was popular in my friend group. I'm also extremely lucky I never had an accident or killed someone.

When the aptitude test results came back, we each paid a visit to the counselor's office to talk about the careers we should consider and the ones we shouldn't. Keep in mind that these weren't based on our IQ or even on what we'd learned in school. It was pure conjecture drawn from how we answered questions about what we liked to do, what we thought we were good at, and what our aspirations were, questions most fifteen-year-olds have scant self-reflective ability to answer.

It was around this time I was desperate to go steady with Lisa Edwards, a cute, blonde, effervescent cheerleader who was the quintessential young man's crush object. She sat in front of me in Algebra, and we had become friendly. I made her laugh. I'm good at that; it's my only superpower. As a result, I figured I had a fighting chance. I had no inkling just how far out of my league she really was.

For those of you under the age of, oh, one hundred, "going steady" was what dating someone exclusively was called back then. You held hands between classes, kissed a little, and went to the movies together, and she wore your letter jacket, if you had one. It often involved a little careful negotiation—no one wanted to face rejection by asking a girl straight-out if she wanted to be your girlfriend. That was a terrifying prospect, even scarier than asking a girl to dance. So you'd typically float the idea to one of her friends to see how the request would be received.

Lisa's best friend was Rebecca, a flame-haired buddy of ours who was as honest as the day is long. Maybe a little too honest, considering I still remember the conversation all these years later.

When we met in front of the school that day after Rebecca had talked to the object of my young heart's yearning desire, she cheerfully let me have it with both barrels.

"She says she really likes you, but you're just too ugly."

Whoever said women are the weaker sex has never been body-slammed through a concrete floor by one.

When the shock wore off a few weeks later I realized it made complete sense. I was a skinny, tow-headed, freckled kid with a nasty scar from a childhood bicycle accident that crawled down my face from the edge of my mouth to my chin. Of course I was too ugly for her! She was Lisa frickin' Edwards, grand prizewinner of the genetic lottery. For the better part of my life I accepted that designation, even after I eventually grew out of the gawky phase. But, stubbornly, I wasn't willing to accept being ignored by the girls I liked. I figured out early on that being funny and smart and charming and confident would go a long way toward getting girls to like me back. That was my theory, anyway. Every once in a great while, it actually worked.

When I sat down in the guidance counselor's office, she took out the computer printout I still have and started down the list of worker trait groups that best matched my test results. Among them were "animal care," "crafts foreman," "technical work," "machine feeding," "modeling (???)," and "messenger/usher."

There was an even longer list of jobs I was evidently over-qualified for, including: "appraise/inspect," "machine set up," and "cashiering." Whew. That was encouraging.

About a month after Rebecca gave me the brutal truth, I was working at Baskin-Robbins (for $1.25 an hour) when the school quarterback and all his lackeys loudly entered. To say I wasn't exactly happy to see them is an understatement. I'd just learned that he—I seem to remember his name was Lee—had just started going steady with, yep, Lisa. Star quarterback dates cheerleader. How cliché.

"Hey, I heard you asked Lisa to be your girlfriend!" he said. "Nice try!" His buddies laughed. Football season was long over, and I had no classes with Lee. The only way he would've known I liked her was if Lisa herself told him. I felt the blood rush to my face. Somehow I kept my mouth shut and set about scooping their orders. When I asked for payment, he leaned forward and said something to the effect of: "How about this one's on the house. You know. Because you love Lisa?"

Ha ha.

The rest is a bit of a blur, except we found ourselves outside on the sidewalk in front of the store, with the all-too-familiar feeling of having a group of unfriendly young men surrounding me as I faced off against a bigger opponent.

"Watch out, Lee," one of his friends yelled. "I heard he knows karate."

I'm not sure what thoughts passed through his head. I was a martial arts novice, still a white belt, who was fifty pounds lighter and more than a few inches shorter than him. This would not be a *Karate Kid* moment. I fully expected to take a beating. But perhaps the slightest possibility of an ignoble defeat by this smaller, uglier loser was too much for Mr. Wonderful to chance.

He threw up his hands and turned away. "C'mon, guys. No bitch is worth fighting for." Swear to God. He said those exact words. I stood there, stunned, as the group headed up the street.

As for the aptitude test's worker trait groups for which I was underqualified, many were, to this day, perfectly accurate. "Accounting." I suck at math. Check. "Engineer." Check. For the same reason. "Legal work." Fairly general description, but okay. "Medical." "Business Consulting." "Surgery." "Scientist." "Production Manager."

Oh yeah. And at the very end of the list of careers I shouldn't even think of considering: "journalist," "creative writing," and "news reporting."

All righty then.

So the next time someone tells you what you can't do, remember these words of T.E. Lawrence: "All men dream, but not equally. Those who dream by night in the dusty recesses of their minds, wake in the day to find that it was vanity: but the dreamers of the day are dangerous men, for they may act on their dreams with open eyes, to make them possible."

CHAPTER 4

THAT TIME I DIED

It was a typical south Texas summer beauty, temperatures in the high eighties, sunshine beating down on my shoulders, pollen from the live oaks covering every surface with a yellow-brown dusting.

I was alone at the community pool in the El Dorado subdivision where I worked as a lifeguard. It was my turn to come in early, clean the pool, and prep everything for the dozens of neighborhood kids who would descend on the place within a few hours. My high school buddies and fellow lifeguards, Steve Girard and Jim Hayes, and a lovely little Latina named Joy I had a secret crush on, were scheduled to show up in about two hours.

Girard was the one who dubbed me "Ghost" at the beginning of the summer. We'd known each other since middle school and had played football and baseball together. I'd just moved back to Texas after a year in Ohio, and my skin was about as white as a sheet of printer paper. Even after I eventually tanned, the nickname stuck. Earlier that year, when I'd finally endured enough lunacy and beatings from my dad and moved into my own apartment, Girard started bringing his weekly conquests over for a little private fun, which meant many nights I would sit in my car, waiting for him to remove the signal sock from the doorknob and take the girl home.

He was a wild man, a brawler, a bar owner who could never edit whatever came out of his big mouth, and I loved him. He died way too soon. As did Jim, a champion triathlete and long-distance swimmer who passed away after a long battle with cancer the same month I began writing this book.

One of my duties that summer day was to vacuum the pool using a long hose attached to the pump system and a pole with a suction device clipped to the end. While cleaning, I noticed an object that seemed to be caught in the drain at the bottom of the deep end. I set the vacuum aside, put on some goggles, and dove in. It was a kid's ball wedged into the grill that covered the drain, held there by the pressure of thirty thousand gallons of water.

I tried wiggling it free, but most of the ball had been sucked into the drain hole. I'd have to take the cover off to retrieve it, so I swam back up and went into the lifeguard office for a screwdriver.

A deep breath, and I was back in the water. The screws holding the grate to the pool bottom were rusted, so after struggling for a bit I decided it would be easier to slip a finger into one of the broken parts of the cover to force the ball out from underneath.

A few seconds later I realized my finger was caught in the grate. I mean really caught. I pulled and pulled and couldn't get it to budge. I'd have to snap the plastic crosspieces to get free. When I reached back for the screwdriver, which was lying on the pool bottom next to me, the action of my hand passing through the water created a wave. The screwdriver rolled out of reach. I swung a leg over to kick it closer, but I only succeeded in sending it even farther away.

My index finger was wedged in up to the second knuckle. I was determined to remain calm, but I was running out of breath. I planted both feet on either side of the grate and heaved with all my might, hoping to at least break the plastic cover to free myself, or to strip enough flesh from around the bone to get loose.

That's the last thing I remember until I woke up sometime later, lying on the edge of the pool. There was no one around. Looking down I could see the cover was still attached to the drain, ball and all. My finger was swollen and sore—but intact.

I lay there for a while, looking up at the blue sky, wondering what had happened.

I still don't know.

CHAPTER 5

KARATE KID

The decrepit Buick station wagon was a faded, scratched, depressing blue, a hue only found in a watercolor painting of the sky that had been thrown out years earlier and was now lying in a landfill, soaking up damaging UV rays. That blue. The paint hadn't seen a wash, and definitely not a wax, in decades.

I kept twirling the dial of the AM/FM radio, hoping to get some kind of halfway decent signal, but whenever I did locate a song, the reception crackled in and out, breaking up the stanzas, turning the lyrics into hiccups of fragmented thoughts. Which was, in a way, the perfect accompaniment to what had become, from the beginning, a bizarre journey.

I was seventeen, and at that point in my life the only thing I was certain about was that I had some talent for punching and kicking people and getting punched and kicked in return. It was about a year earlier that my dad had smacked me in the head one too many times for some minor issue I can't even remember, and I gave him a piston-shot to the chest, which drove him back into the wall. His eyes widened in shock. I packed a bag and left home.

The man driving the Buick was my sensei, Wan Pae Pak, a seventh Dan karate master. It would not have surprised me if George Lucas someday admitted his Star Wars character Yoda was modeled after Master Pak. He was short, stooped, and enigmatic, with a wizened face and lightning-quick hands. He always wore his starched, blindingly white *gi*. I never saw him in any other clothes. No one knew exactly how old he was, and he liked it that way. All any of his students were told was that he immigrated from South Korea while a teenage boy and had never quite conquered all the nuances of the English language.

We were halfway back to San Antonio after I had competed in the Grand National Tae Kwon Do Championships in Des Moines, Iowa. Four days earlier, we'd taken the same route up, completing the fifteen-hour journey in a single run. I think Master Pak said a total of ten words the entire trip. We shared a Days Inn room to save money. He preferred McDonald's over Burger King.

I was representing Texas in the competition. That might be why Master Pak decided to accompany me personally. It was a great honor to his dojo for one of his students to be invited. The tournament was under the jurisdiction of Chung Do Kwan, a presiding body based in South Korea. The scoring system was simple: one point for a hand strike, two for a foot strike. It was controlled contact: combatants were penalized for not pulling their shots. You were allowed to do some damage—just not kill or cripple your opponent.

I made it to the semifinals in my level and ended up facing one of the top fighters in the country. He was wiry, taller than me, and graceful as hell. Within the first minute it became obvious his foot technique was flawless. At one point he shot a kick past my head, and just as I moved in for a punch, thinking he'd missed, he snapped his heel into the back of my head. Blood arched from my nose in slow motion. I stumbled forward and managed to land a fist to his chest, but it took me a few minutes of dancing around, out of his reach, to recover my wits. "Two points!" the scoring ref shouted.

In contrast to my opponent, my foot technique was pathetic. Mainly because I have the tightest hamstrings in the world. Master Pak took to leaning his full weight on my back during my stretches to try and get the damn things to lengthen, which was, as you might imagine, exquisite torture. In that particular tournament, fighters were required to successfully land a certain number of kicks or suffer a penalty. In my earlier matches I threw just enough to not be disqualified, but the vast percentage of my points were achieved through hand strikes. I was simply faster than the other contestants.

As the fight went on, I was thumping the guy pretty well, landing stiff shots to his chest and sides. Punches to the face weren't allowed, although kicks were. But I began to realize that the referee, who came to Des Moines direct from Seoul earlier that week specifically to work the Nationals, was not throwing up his hand and call out a score whenever I made contact. Unsure of what to do, I started punching harder to demonstrate to him that I was, in fact, making good strikes. But he continued to ignore them.

Master Pak, standing at the edge of the fighting mat, began shouting at the referee, who took exception to something said to him in Korean and issued a warning. When the fight ended, it was the other guy's hand raised in triumph. Don't get me wrong—he was good. But I knew I'd hit him six times as much as he hit me.

"He old school," Master Pak said, pointing to the ref. "No like hand technique. Only foot. Come." He strode past the officials' desk, haranguing them in his own language the entire time. I hurried to catch up. "Are we going to stay and watch the final match?" I asked. He shook his head and pointed to one of the ridiculously tall, gleaming trophies next to the judges. "That fourth place. That not you. If we take, it mean we agree. We do not agree."

We left the convention center, got in the Buick, and started south.

Somewhere in the middle of Kansas, I finally zeroed in on a crystal-clear country-music station. Kenny Rogers was giving advice about how to play poker.

Master Pak brightened up and began singing along at the top of his voice. In perfect English.

CHAPTER 6

BREAKFAST WITH THE MICK

I recognized him the moment the door opened, and he slid onto the barstool. His face, puffed up a bit by age and alcohol, was still one of the most beloved in the world. Mickey Mantle wasn't just an American idol, he *was* America.

He greeted me with a warm grin. "Hey there, barkeep. Still serving breakfast?" It was barely eleven in the morning. There was no one else in the bar.

Somehow I sputtered an answer. "No sir, sorry, kitchen won't open until five."

"Goddamn that's good news. Then I'll have a brandy, Kahlúa, and cream."

I learned years later that's what the Mick called his "breakfast of champions."

He was born in Oklahoma in 1931. His parents, Mutt and Lovell, named him after Hall of Fame catcher Mickey Cochrane, so it's no stretch to say baseball was a part of his life from the moment he first opened his eyes. He batted left-handed when his father pitched to him, and right-handed when his grandfather did, and he eventually became the only major league player in history to hit 150 home runs from both sides of the plate. He is indisputably considered one of the greatest ballplayers ever, and perhaps the best switch hitter to ever pick up a bat. I could go on and on about his historic stats, but if you're a baseball fan, you already know them, and if you're not, you won't appreciate them.

I can't remember why he was in Dallas that day—perhaps for a memorabilia convention, or maybe he was scheduled to comment on a game—but it looked as though he had time to kill. He stayed on that barstool for three hours, telling me stories, cracking jokes, making me pinch myself every few minutes to make sure it wasn't a dream. He switched from "breakfast" to Scotch to wine and kept talking. There was a moment when I hesitated with the bottle poised over his empty glass, and he waved a dismissive hand and said in his Okie drawl, "I've got a car coming. Don't worry. Ain't drivin' myself nowheres."

"I never drank before a game," I recall him saying. "Except one time when I was on the injured list and didn't think they'd put me in. Called on me to pitch hit, goddamn it. Can you believe it?" Hungover, possibly even still drunk, he managed to crush a home run to left field, tying the game with Baltimore. When Mickey Mantle told his stories, you couldn't help but sense he was amazed as anyone over his abilities and good fortune. He was modest and plainspoken. There was nothing fake about him at all. Years later I watched an interview where he lamented not taking better care of himself. "It was stupid," he said, telling younger athletes. "You only get one body, and don't mess it up."

When I told the lifetime Yankee that my father worshipped him, I could've sworn he blushed.

Dad was a good ballplayer in his own right, even getting invited to a tryout for the Chicago Cubs as a catcher. He played a few years as a semipro before enlisting in the Air Force. Somehow that came up in our conversation, and the Mick talked with affection about his own dad, how close they were—"No boy ever loved his father more," he once said—how they played catch any chance they could; how his parents saved his career by driving through the night to a hospital in

Oklahoma City to get an experimental drug, penicillin, saving his infected leg from being amputated when he was still a boy.

I deliberately didn't tell him about my own experience with sports and my father, how I couldn't remember him ever throwing a ball with me or going to my Little League or high school football or tennis games. I suspect it galled my dad that I wasn't as good a baseball player as he was, so he just never showed any interest.

When the bar started filling up in the early afternoon, Mantle drained his glass and asked what he owed me. "It's on me," I replied. "This has been one of the best days of my life." He graciously thanked me, got up a little unsteadily, and walked out to his waiting limo. A few years later, I—and the rest of the baseball world—was saddened to hear he died of cancer, likely caused by decades of alcohol abuse, which had already taken the lives of two of his sons. I can't deny that I contributed to that, albeit in a small way, and I regret to this day not cutting him off sooner. When he passed away in 1995, he was the same age I am now.

Before he left the bar, he grabbed a cocktail napkin and asked for a pen. "To Don," he wrote, "My best wishes. Mickey Mantle." I framed it, with a photo of the Mick in his prime, and told my dad the great man had signed it for him (I'm named after my father). He proudly displayed it on his living room wall until he died of Alzheimer's many years later.

CHAPTER 7

THE BIG BREAK

"I've got a job for you when you graduate." That was what the former executive producer of KENS's evening newscast told me after he tracked my phone number down. "Pack your bags and come to High Point."

Jack Moore was a bullying, bragging, brilliant, larger-than-life personality who happened to spot something in this twenty-three-year-old unpaid intern. I was just weeks away from an associate's degree in radio, television, and film from San Antonio College (I'd go on to earn a bachelor's in history from UNCC a few years later) and had no idea what to do next. Jack's call opened up the world to me.

High Point, North Carolina, is a bit of a misnomer. When Jack first mentioned it, I'd pictured a mountain town somewhere in the Blue Ridge; in fact, it was built on fairly flat land between Greensboro and Winston-Salem. It got its name from having the highest elevation on the train line that passes through. Yes, this Colorado boy was initially disappointed, but nonetheless High Point became heaven to me, and my years there were ones of learning my craft, growing my confidence, and enjoying numerous friendships.

Jack Moore was the new news director for the ABC (now FOX) affiliate in the Piedmont Triad, as the combined three-city television market is called. The original facility took up a few floors of the old Sheraton Hotel in the middle of town. Its studios were converted from the once-opulent ballroom. He had a tiny staff and tinier budget.

I loaded up everything I could fit into my little brown Datsun 260Z, which wasn't much, and headed north. Two days later I pulled into the sleepy little town that called itself the "Furniture Capital of the World" and found the station. Jack greeted me at the door and gave me the very brief tour of the facilities before we sat down in his office. He reached into a desk drawer, pulled out a gas card and a set of car keys, and tossed both to me.

"Pick out a camera to use in the engineering room," he said in his characteristic growl, adding, "Not one of the new ones."

"OK. But what exactly am I doing?"

He laughed. "Telling stories, you idiot."

That was the start of three and a half years of the best job I've ever had.

My beat was pretty much anywhere I could get to in the ancient Dodge van that I found parked in the station lot behind the hotel. As the "Tar Heel Traveler" (the brand Jack came up with), I was responsible for shooting, writing, editing, and voicing two or three pieces a week about the interesting, entertaining, inspiring people of the Carolinas. Fiddle makers. Artists. Moonshiners. Fishermen. Civil War reenactors. I had no expense account. I slept in the back of the van and bought snacks and drinks with the gas card.

And I learned how to tell stories.

To this day I have no idea why Jack gave me that job. There were plenty of other, more experienced journalists at WGHP and elsewhere. But I'm grateful as hell he did. He paid me an annual salary of $10,000 to be the happiest working stiff on the planet.

My role model for the *Tar Heel Traveler* was the legendary CBS correspondent and *Sunday Morning* anchor Charles Kuralt. His *On the Road* segments were the gold standard for television feature reporting. Beautifully shot and written, they introduced America to itself—he best of itself. I didn't have his silky baritone pipes, but I could try to capture the essence of his writing, and that's what I worked most on. Kuralt used a minimum of words, but they were perfectly chosen. In contrast, he used a maximum of natural sounds and stirring pictures, many of which were shot by his equally legendary cameraman, Isadore Bleckman. Many years later I had the joy and honor of working on a *Sunday Morning* piece with Izzy in the Atchafalaya Basin of Louisiana. We spent a few glorious days paddling around the bayous together. Sadly, he passed away in 2021.

Jack Moore gave me complete freedom to choose the subjects of my stories. He or the show producer would go over my scripts with the lightest touch, allowing me to develop my own style and voice. That would never happen today. There were times when I came back with nothing more than an essay with images I'd collected along the way to other stories: a paean to small town murals, or covered bridges, or autumn. *"Nothing gold can stay, said Robert Frost...."*

Neither can, it turns out, the best job.

When Jack was fired after a confrontation with police over some teenagers he thought were threatening his son, a new sheriff came to town: Gary Curtis. Curtis was a former television anchor turned news director who had a massive chip on his shoulder. Why, no one could ever figure out. But he ruled the newsroom with an iron fist and loud temper. He reminded me of my father.

Three days into his reign I was driving to the mountains for a story about an elderly woman who made whimsical creations out of gourds when I heard a police call come over the scanner that was still mounted to the dash of my van. SWAT teams were being dispatched to a hostage situation about a mile from where I was. I radioed back to the station to say I was close by and would shoot whatever video I could at the scene until another news crew could pitch up.

I found the address, parked next door, pulled out my camera, climbed down next to the unmarked van, and began shooting video. Police units were still streaming into the neighborhood. Barricades were being set up. Other members of the news media with their rolling billboards were held at bay down the block. I was the only one inside the frozen zone, unseen by the authorities.

I watched an armed figure pass by the window. Police negotiators were talking to him over a bullhorn. My car radio crackled. It was the assignment editor.

"Where are you?" she asked.

"Thirty feet away. I can see everything."

"Stand by. We're going live. We have a microwave truck with a camera outside the police line pointed at you. Use the two-way radio to talk." (This was before the days of cell phones.)

For the next two hours, I described what I could see on live television. When the crisis was finally peacefully resolved and the gunman hauled away without incident, I signed off, hopped back in the van, and started on my way to the mountains.

The radio crackled again. It was Curtis.

"Great job. Come back to the station."

"But I have a shoot scheduled."

"Not anymore. Get your ass back here."

Thirty minutes later he told me the *Tar Heel Traveler* was no more. I was to be his primary hard-news nightside reporter.

I didn't want to do that. I told him so. I loved my job. People loved those stories.

"I don't care," he snarled back. "You do what I say you do."

"Then I quit," I said. I got up and walked out of the station without even bothering to clean out my desk.

Yes, it was a stupid thing to do. I had no other job prospects. Not much money in the bank. And Curtis had every right to reassign his employee.

But it pissed me off. It wouldn't be the last time I walked away from a paying gig on principle. Some people never learn. And by "some people," I'm referring to me.

A few freelance writing jobs kept the rent paid and ramen noodles on the table until I finally joined up with an organization in Richmond, Virginia, the Foreign Mission Board, that was doing exciting documentary work all over the world. I drove up to Richmond in an ice storm so bad I had to creep along at three miles an hour with two wheels off the side of the road to maintain traction. My Volkswagen Beetle's springs were pushed flat by the weight of the ice that coated it four inches thick.

After our initial interview, Van Payne, the head of the film/video department, hired me.

"Would you like some constructive feedback?" he asked.

"Sure."

"You come across as a little overconfident in your abilities."

So noted. That was the first of a great many things I learned from Van.

It was the start of a whole new chapter of international travel and filmmaking, one that eventually led to the opportunity to make a documentary with the man whose work I've admired my entire life, the man whose writing style I emulated, the man whose storytelling skills are, to this day, unmatched: my role model from my *Tar Heel Traveler* days, Charles Kuralt. Sometimes life can be stunningly circular.

Kuralt and the famed musician and songwriter Loonis McGlohon were making a video version of their popular recording about their beloved home state for broadcast on public television, and they hired me and Van to shoot it.

We traveled almost every inch of North Carolina, interviewing people, waiting for the perfect light for the perfect shot of wildflowers or old barns or newborn colt or snow fall-ing on a mountain stream. It took us the better part of a year; a weekend here, a handful of days there, whenever Charles could break away from his day job with CBS. My favorite memory, however, was sitting in a restaurant in Duck, North Carolina, as we sat drinking vodka with the owner.

After regaling us with stories about his time on the road, Charles, slightly tipsy, turned to me. "You're still young, so take this for what it's worth."

I awaited his words of wisdom as he took a sip of his drink. Would he tell me how to become a network correspondent? How to rise to the highest levels of broadcast news? How to craft the perfect sentence?

No. In his inimitable deep drawl, the great man announced, "Don, my only regret in life"—a pause, a tilt of the head, a grin—"is not having more sex."

CHAPTER 8

END OF AN EMPIRE

The Soviet Union was in the midst of a slow collapse. After the fall of the Berlin Wall, the empire's was only a matter of time. Statues of Lenin and Stalin were being torn down in various cities. Protesters took to Red Square, complaining of the low standard of living, lack of food, and absence of goods on the shelves of GUM, the iconic department store.

The first night there, I had just finished taking a shower when a knock sounded at the door. I wrapped a towel around my waist and answered. Two women stood before me, dressed in cocktail attire and a little too much makeup. One was probably in her late thirties or forties; the other looked eighteen at most. The older woman reached over and grabbed me under the towel. "Sex," she said. "Dollars." The younger girl smiled and winked. I thanked them and, holding tightly to my modesty as well as the towel, backed away and shut the door.

That was perhaps the clearest sign that Russia was undergoing a massive change. Hotel Metropol security would have never let prostitutes up to the tourist floors in the past, unless, I suppose, the KGB was videotaping the encounter for extortion purposes.

A few days later, Van Payne and I were on what seemed a never-ending twenty-six-hour-long train ride through the Russian countryside, en route to Kazakhstan. At every stop along the way, elderly female wheeltappers would walk alongside the train, pinging the wheels with a long hammer to test their integrity. Unfortunately, they did so regardless of the time of night. Three times a day, the soup lady wheeled her cart through the narrow passageway, selling whatever the meal of the day was. God forbid you had a foot or arm hanging outside the doorway to your tiny berth when she was motoring past. The soup or stew could sometimes be questionable, but the fresh-baked bread was divine.

Later that week, we found ourselves at the Baikonur Cosmodrome, home of the Soviet space program. We were there to film the very first launch of a Kazakh cosmonaut, Toktar Aubakirov, for a documentary about his home country. Security there, too, was much more relaxed than we were expecting. Our press credentials had been easily acquired, and when we asked where we could set up our camera for the launch, the media liaison waved a hand in the general direction of the Soyuz rocket and mumbled, "Anywhere over there, but if you go past that fence you will be burned to a crisp by the blast." We chose a spot considerably farther away than the fence. Even so, we could feel the blistering heat from the rocket engine as the ground shook beneath our feet.

We didn't know it at the time, but that was the last Soviet mission to space.

CHAPTER 9

THERE ARE MORE THINGS IN HEAVEN AND EARTH...

The sun on my back was hot and heavy, a discernable weight, as I walked near the village of Sanwabo in Burkina Faso, following a narrow footpath through the scrub. Suddenly there was movement on the ground to my right, and I spotted a brightly colored green mamba snake about ten feet away just as he shot forward, aiming directly for me. I barely had time to leap into the air as he passed underneath my boots and into the tuft of grass. Mambas are some of the fastest snakes in Africa, and also among the most poisonous. It was a good fifteen minutes before my heart rate returned to normal.

Van Payne and I were in West Africa to film some well-digging operations funded by a Christian charity group, and in my rare downtime I liked to go on walkabouts. One day as I strolled along, I began hearing singing and chanting up ahead. Rounding a curve in the path, I came upon a tiny village of just a handful of mud-and-straw houses covered in strikingly beautiful geometric designs. About two dozen people were swaying and chanting in unison in what appeared to be a communal area as an elderly man in the center spoke in a loud voice. His hand was pressed to the forehead of a young woman of about twenty years of age whose eyes were closed. Her body was shaking as if she were in some sort of seizure, and her white dress was drenched in sweat. As I watched, the woman suddenly shrieked and fell to the ground, gyrating and convulsing. The man standing over her shouted something in the local dialect, and the young woman immediately fell still.

Four or five of the onlookers then gently picked her up and carried the unconscious girl into one of the houses. Just then the man who had been conducting the ceremony spotted me, smiled, and walked over. In halting English, he asked who I was and what I was doing there. I told him and he seemed pleased. So I asked him what was it I just witnessed.

"She was a witch," he explained. "I cast the demon out of her. She will be fine now."

CHAPTER 10

THONGS FOR THE MEMORIES

It was around noon in Nairobi on a beautiful, blue-sky day. I was walking through the Maasai market, where tourists can buy trinkets, colorfully dyed batik fabrics, and intricate Makonde soapstone or ebony carvings, when I paused at a crosswalk. Dozens of people milled around me as we waited for a break in traffic. Suddenly I felt something hard press into the middle of my back, and from directly behind me a voice said, "Give me your bag." The traffic light changed, and the crowd shuffled forward, many glancing at the gun, the robber, and me, before continuing on across the street. Ho hum. Just another day in Kenya's capital city.

The man was in his midtwenties. He wore an Aerosmith T-shirt, shorts, flip-flops, and dark shades. With the non-gun-holding hand he directed me over to a less-crowded part of the sidewalk. "Give me your money and your bag," he repeated. It was apparent to me he wasn't the slightest bit concerned someone would raise an alarm.

I was in town for just a few days before heading to a project in South Africa about education and sanitation efforts in Soweto. In my backpack I had my personal camera, some credit cards, a few thousand Kenya shillings, about $10,000 in American Express Travelers Cheques, and two passports. It was foolish to leave valuables in one's hotel room. As for why I had two perfectly good passports—back then, in the late '80s, international travel was problematic if you happened to pass through South Africa or Israel and get a stamp in your passport. South Africa was a pariah state because of its apartheid policies; Israel was controversial to many Middle Eastern governments because of its treatment of the Palestinians. Quite a few nations, in protest of their policies, would reject anyone bearing proof of travel to those places at the border. So those of us whose job it was to occasionally work in one or both of those countries often carried two passports. It was completely legal. All it took was a letter explaining the situation and a copy of a purchased plane ticket showing one's upcoming travels, and the US Passport Agency would issue a valid little blue book strictly for use in those shunned countries.

"Take the money and the camera," I told the robber. "But I need my passports."

"Nah, *mzungu*. I'll take it all." He pulled the backpack off my shoulder, stuck the pistol back into his waistband, and sauntered away. *Mzungu* is the Swahili term that originally meant "wanderer" but that came to be somewhat derogatory slang for "white man," especially tourists. I bit down the impulse to yell after him that I was no tourist; I'd spent months at a time all over the continent.

An apathetic police officer jotted down my account before waving me away from his desk. The folks at the American embassy were sympathetic and helpful as they put in an emergency request for a replacement passport. American Express said the replacement cheques would be issued as soon as they received a copy of the police complaint. Both offices had a lot of practice with my situation. Nairobi's crime rate and the blatant daytime robberies of foreigners were a national embarrassment. Today, it's only getting worse, and regular Kenyans are the ones suffering most.

Fortunately, because I had a credit card number on file, I wasn't kicked out of my hotel despite my sudden lack of liquidity and could charge my dinners to the room until the replacement travelers cheques arrived. These were the days before Venmo or Zelle, or even cell phones and electronic banking.

About a week later I got a message at the front desk that my crisp, new American passport was ready. The embassy also gave me an official letter explaining why it had no entry stamp, which would otherwise have raised suspicions when I tried to leave Kenya. There was one complication to continuing my journey on to Johannesburg: the visa stamp was in my stolen passport, and there was no South African consulate in Kenya (or almost all of Africa, for that matter) to issue a replacement. In fact, the only nation on the entire continent that had diplomatic relations with South Africa was Malawi.

Commercial flights to Lilongwe, Malawi's capital, were infrequent, so I hired a bush pilot who'd been recommended by a friend. The next morning we loaded up my cases of video gear and took off from Jomo Kenyatta Airport in his twin-engine Cessna. Before he started the engine, the pilot (I have long since forgotten his name) repeatedly heaved down on the nose of the aircraft to see how slowly or quickly the tail returned to rest, testing if the weight of my equipment presented a risk.

"Are you concerned about taking off?" I asked as he climbed aboard.

His laconic reply was classic Humphrey Bogart: "Taking off ain't the problem. I've got extra fuel tanks built in back there. We're tail heavy. It's being able to nose her down that's got me wondering."

"Wondering...about landing?"

"Oh hell," he chuckled, firing up the starter. "Landing is guaranteed. One way or another, we will return to earth."

That wasn't exactly reassuring.

The spectacular thing about Nairobi is its proximity to thousands and thousands of acres of Savannah. As soon as we left the ground, I could see grassy plains beneath us, with herds of wildlife seemingly stretching from horizon to horizon.

We flew due south, passing relatively slow and low over public and private wildlife reserves. With autopilot engaged, my travel companion slipped on his reading glasses and cracked open a book. When the sloping profile of Mount Kilimanjaro appeared off our left wing, marking the border with Tanzania, he sat forward and made a slight course correction before returning to the adventures of Dirk Pitt. I think he only looked up one more time during that trip, flipping a lever to switch to the reserve gas tanks. I spent the entire journey peering down at wildebeest and giraffes, antelopes, and elephants.

It took about four hours, if I remember correctly, but eventually we spotted the long, squat terminal and adjacent runways of Kamuzu International Airport. The pilot radioed in for permission, throttled back, and started our descent. "Here goes nothing," he muttered, forgetting that I could hear him in my headphones. Or maybe he didn't forget.

Fortunately, the Cessna obeyed like a well-trained horse and dipped its nose before eventually easing its landing gear gently onto the tarmac.

There were eager porters waiting to carry my heavy cases to customs, where officials spent an inordinate amount of time looking through my personal items for contraband. One of the armed men approached me with a ruler and actually measured the length of my hair. I was expecting that.

For lack of a better description, Malawi was a bizarre place. Since gaining independence from the United Kingdom in 1964, it had become a totalitarian state under its unwonted dictator, Hastings Banda, who was still president well into his eighties by the time I visited. A British-trained medical doctor, Banda was eccentric and overbearing, to say the least. Phones were systematically tapped, and if anyone was overheard saying anything at all critical of him, the call was cut off.

Mail was routinely opened and inspected. "Everything is my business," he famously declared. "Everything. Anything I say is law. Literally anything." There was no opposition; at least, none that survived. Three cabinet members who expressed support of a multiparty democracy mysteriously died in a "traffic accident." In reality, they were tortured and the accident staged. An autopsy later showed they had all been killed by tent stakes hammered into their heads. Years later the dictator was put on trial for those murders but acquitted for lack of evidence. Dead men don't tell tales.

In Banda's Malawi, every building was required to prominently feature his portrait, and no other picture or clock could be mounted higher. Movie theaters had to play a video of their president waving at the audience before the film could start. Books on pre-Banda African history were burned. Newspapers were censored.

A self-proclaimed conservative Christian, Banda forbade same-sex relationships. Women couldn't wear trousers or skirts higher than their knees, and all beards and mustaches were banned for men. During my airport inspection, if my hair had been longer than my shirt collar, the customs officials were authorized to give me a haircut or see that I was put on the next plane out.

Somehow, I passed muster and was permitted into the country. It took two cabs to shuttle me and my gear to a hotel in downtown Lilongwe.

In striking contrast to their leader, Malawians are considered some of the warmest and friendliest people in Africa. My week there confirmed that to me. Everyone was cheerful and helpful and very, very curious about the rare foreigner in their midst. After all, Malawi wasn't exactly the tourist capital of the continent. As with a lot of totalitarian states, crime was almost nonexistent, if you didn't count political assassinations. I walked around freely without concern while the South African consulate took its sweet time processing my visa application. God forbid they let just anyone into their racist, oppressive, antidemocratic country. Standards must be upheld. References checked. Articles or broadcasts I'd made pored over for anything I said that could be construed as critical of the white regime.

With time to kill, I hired a guide to take me to Lake Malawi on a scouting trip, hoping to eventually get funding to make a nature film about its waters, which team with colorful fish. My proposal, eventually rejected by *National Geographic*, was to focus specifically on the 850 or so species of a type of fish called "cichlids" found there, and how they represent evolution at a stunningly increased rate. One of their more interesting traits is an ability to change their sex when the situation demands. I'm relatively certain President Banda would have declared such spontaneous transgenderism illegal. But I found it fascinating. Another example of nature finding a way.

On the fifth day, I had finished reading the two books I'd taken with me and successfully explored pretty much every part of the city. With television banned for all but the wealthiest citizens—who watched smuggled VHS tapes, as there were no broadcasts in the entire country—the only source of public entertainment was the local movie theater. That day the marquee announced it would be showing *Crocodile Dundee* in thirty minutes, so I bought a ticket, which cost less than a dollar in local currency, and went inside the blissfully cool theater.

It didn't take long for the room to begin filling up. People who sat near me all leaned over to say hi to the stranger in their midst.

Here's the thing about movies in Malawi: before they're allowed to be shown to the public, all films are first reviewed by the Censorship Board. Politics, references to communism, nudity, and any other socially unacceptable behavior, including kissing, were routinely and inelegantly edited out. Once it was determined nothing objectionable remained, the reels of film were given a sticker of suitability and returned to the theater owner.

I'd seen *Crocodile Dundee* when it first arrived in the States a few years prior. I remembered some, uh, interesting scenes in it, and I was curious as to how the censors would deal with those crucial moments in the plot.

The tattered curtain was cranked open, the president waved at us from the screen as the national anthem played, and the movie began. No coming attractions preceded it—we were all thrown straight in to reporter Sue Charlton, played by Linda Kozlowski, venturing off to Australia in pursuit of a story about the eponymous living legend, played by Paul Hogan. All good so far, except the projectionist had mistakenly used the wrong lens—cinemascope, perhaps, instead of standard. The top and bottom two feet of the picture were cut off, leaving some characters on screen headless. It was a bit disconcerting, but my fellow audience members didn't seem to mind.

Now, there's a moment in the movie you may recall when Kozlowski and Hogan are traveling through the bush to the site of his famous battle with a gigantic crocodile. It's hot. They're dirty and tired. So that clueless city-dwelling New York reporter, Sue Charlton, naturally strips down to her underwear for a dip in the crocodile-infested river. I mean, who wouldn't, right?

Knowing what was coming, I was expecting this to be the first chop job by the censors. I was wrong. Perhaps they had all taken a bathroom break at that exact moment, but suddenly we were all looking up at Linda Kozlowski's magnificent ass, all ten feet of it on the big screen, sporting a tiny black thong as she waded delicately into the muddy water.

You would've thought someone had just fired off a gun. The entire audience jumped as fifty pairs of butt cheeks clinched in unison at the same moment. Women screamed.

Men shouted. I thought there was going to be a riot. For a moment I feared for the life of the projectionist.

But then, a few seconds later, a smattering of chuckles spread throughout the room. Then outright laughter. Then applause. The audience settled back into their seats, chattering away; relieved, I'm sure, that in having seen the forbidden fruit, no one spontaneously combusted or went blind. To this day I can't scroll past that movie on cable without thinking of that moment.

I ultimately made it to South Africa and finished the project. As I was showing the lady at the Lilongwe departure gate my ticket, she asked if I had enjoyed my stay in Malawi. "Very much," I answered. "Interesting laws you have here."

"Oh?" she replied guilelessly. "Are they not the same as your country?"

I just smiled and got on the plane. By the way, in 2011 the man who succeeded Banda as president signed a law making public farting illegal. Now there's a piece of legislation I can get behind.

CHAPTER 11

GOODBYE, CALCUTTA

The knock on the hotel door came just after 3:00 a.m. It took me a few minutes to wake up and clear my head, wondering if I'd really heard what I thought I heard. Then there was more knocking, more urgently than before, and a voice calling out my name.

It was Sri, our fixer and translator. I've changed his name for reasons that will become obvious. When I opened the door he stepped inside, nervously glancing back down the hallway before closing the door.

"I'm so sorry to bother you this early, but my brother [a police officer in Calcutta] warned me that they are about to raid this hotel and confiscate all of your films. They will arrest you."

The gig was up. Time to leave.

Joanna Pinneo, a wonderfully skilled photographer, and I had been in Calcutta for the past month. She was taking stills for a magazine article; I was filming a documentary about one of the oldest and largest cities in the world. To keep costs down and our profile low, I was producer, cameraman, soundman, and writer on the project.

"We'll be ready to go in an hour," I said. He nodded and left.

India is not the easiest place for a journalist to work. The government is, to this day, suspicious of reporters from other countries. Understandable, I guess, considering the decades of bad ink about corruption, poverty, crime, and the caste system. But we weren't there to just point out the bad things; we were there to tell the story of what life was like for the people who lived in West Bengal. Even so, we almost didn't get in.

For months I'd been writing the consulate, requesting permission to film in Calcutta. The responses were, in their inscrutably Indian way, polite but vague: "Thank you for your interest. We are pleased to assure you this request is being considered. We will inform you of our decision soon."

Soon, in India, actually means "interminable."

Our passports contained valid tourist visas. But there was no way I could get ten cases of film gear into the country without authorization. It was already early April. Letter after letter was met with similar platitudes, similar delays. The rainy season was approaching. As the weeks went by, my hopes of getting there and filming in May, before the monsoons hit, were dimming. Another month came and went, and then another.

"Yes, Mr. Dahler. We are grateful for your interest in filming in India. We will no doubt have your permits together soon. Thank you for your patience."

This is, of course, a vast characterization, but it occurred to me that Indians have a difficult time just saying no. So they ever so nicely put you off, and put you off, and put you off, until you ultimately get the message. Finally, in mid-July, I'd just about given up. The latest letter from the consulate was two pages long, the first containing more assurances that everything was moving along nicely and that I would have good news any day now, but as of now, I did not have permission; and the second, also bearing the national seal of India and a letterhead, was a cheerful list of answers to my specific questions about whether an insurance carnet is required for the film equipment and whether we would be assigned a government minder to work with us. Yes and no, the helpful bureaucrat explained at length. That page was signed at the bottom and stamped.

I looked at it closely and read it again. It dawned on me that particular page could pass as a stand-alone document. It had the letterhead, the official stamp, and the signature. The responses to my questions could be interpreted as an affirmation that our visit was already approved. The key word being *interpreted*.

I tore off the first page, tossed it away, and called Joanna to tell her to book a flight and get packed. What was the worst that could happen? We'd get turned away at the airport in Bombay (now Mumbai) and sent back home? I was willing to take that risk.

There's a good reason why the Middle English root of the word *travel* is *travail*. Only rarely do things go perfectly well.

Swissair. New York to Zurich. Somewhere en route, the airline lost a crucial equipment case. It took three days for officials to track it down at the Charles de Gaulle airport in Paris while we chilled our heels in Switzerland. How and why it ended up there no one could explain. They vowed to forward it to our final destination, and I had no choice but to take their word for it. On to India we went.

We landed in Bombay late at night. The customs official looked at our stack of black Pelican cases with wide eyes. I showed him the insurance carnet and grandly presented him with the letter from the consulate. He carefully read both, handed them back, and declared we did not have the correct documentation to enter the country with that gear. I politely asked if I could speak with his superior. "He will not be here until tomorrow at noon."

"OK," I replied. "We'll wait."

Jo and I settled down onto the floor next to our mound of baggage. The airport had no air conditioning, and even though it was the middle of the night, the air was stiflingly warm and very muggy. Other than a few janitors, some armed guards, and the sole customs official, we were the only people there. We both faded in and out of sleep.

At about 4:00 a.m. there was a slight commotion. I looked up to see the customs official greeting another man dressed similarly, then walk away. The new man settled into the desk chair and shuffled some papers. I stood and walked over.

"Good morning!" I said cheerfully. He smiled and returned the greeting. A good sign, I thought. "We're from America and waiting to get on the next flight to Calcutta."

He looked over at Jo and the pile. "And all that is your luggage? What is in it?"

"Film equipment. We're making a movie about the people of Calcutta."

He nodded and walked over to the cases, pointing at random ones. "Please open that one." The official looked through stacks of video cords, microphones, batteries, and such, then asked to see what was in a few more. Finally, evidently satisfied we weren't smuggling any contraband, he said, "May I see your passports and documents, please?"

I handed them to him, holding my breath. He read over everything carefully and picked up the phone on his desk, saying a few words in Marathi before hanging up.

"The porters will be here shortly to help you get over to the departure terminal," he said with a smile. "Have a nice visit." With a flourish he stamped our passports and the second page of the letter. It took everything I had to not let my incredulity show. Thank God those were the days before computers and smartphones, or with one stroke of a key he would have seen that our authorization was little more than a wish and a bluff.

The ancient 707 wheezed and bounced down the runway at 6:00 a.m. We were squeezed into incredibly small seats, making the three-hour flight a special kind of torture. Before the doors had closed and pilot began his multilingual preflight instructions, I was expecting a few angry officials to show up and escort us off the plane, but no one ever did.

Jo and I were already exhausted, sleep deprived, and bruised from our journey, and the real work hadn't even started yet. My journal entry from the day we finally set foot in Calcutta:

> One word comes to mind as we rode [sic] the packed mini-van from the airport to the New Kenilworth Hotel...*mold*. The air is moldy. The buildings moldy. The car seats, the towels, the food, the water, the light bulbs...all green with mold. The city has an ancient feel about it, like some old beast half decayed waiting to breathe its last. It doesn't help matters much that the monsoons are still hanging around, dumping brown rain on rich and poor daily. Humidity hovers at 99–100%, rain or no, and breathing is not unlike sucking on a wet blanket. No, it's not a pleasant place, not at this time of year, anyway. But I wasn't expecting Monte Carlo either. Calcutta's charms are in her people and her history.

We checked into the hotel, went to our separate rooms— which were deliciously cool thanks to modern air conditioning—and collapsed into deep sleep until the next morning. The missing case arrived later that afternoon. Tip of the hat to Swissair.

The keys to a good story, be it novel, movie, or documentary, are compelling characters, ones to care about, root for, or despise. Sri had found the perfect family to act as the micro to the macro story of the old city.

Their names were Kartik and Kamala Singh. He earned about three dollars a day pulling a rickshaw through the crowded, chaotic streets, while she cared for their three small children and one scrawny pet chicken. Their home was a black plastic lean-to on a small square of sidewalk for which Kartik paid monthly rent. Given the crushing poverty that gripped the entire state of West Bengal, the family was considered lower middle class. That slab of concrete had been their home for fifteen years. It's hard to imagine, but they were fortunate. Every night, tens of thousands, if not more—mainly men— stretched out like firewood on the sidewalks of Calcutta to sleep, without the luxury of a plastic tent or even a blanket.

Jo and I settled into a routine of starting at the crack of dawn, 4:30 a.m., to get footage of the family as they started their day and scenes around the city before it grew too crowded and the midday light harshened. We filmed and photographed the Singhs together as they eat breakfast, then either stayed with Kamala for a bit as the mother played with her kids and gave lessons or broke away with Kartik on his rickshaw rounds. On days when it rained, the streets filled up with water quickly, and Kartik's rickshaw was in high demand, with its tall wheels and seat set high above the murky floods. The more it rained, the more money he made. I watched him haul customers through waist-deep water that taxis couldn't ford.

On occasion, a passerby would take offense at the two Westerners filming on their streets and raise a noisy ruckus. I couldn't understand what was being said, but I assumed they were embarrassed by the poverty and filth and didn't want us to show that to the rest of the world. With so many unemployed people milling about with nothing better to do, the shouting would quickly attract a crowd. At those times our work was pretty much done for the day, for better or worse, so we'd pack up and head back to the hotel, or to another part of the city to shoot scenics. Only once did someone turn violent; a middle-aged man grabbed me and my camera as I was filming Kartik preparing dinner and yelled for me to stop. He insisted that we were taking pictures of those "beggars" (he was of a higher caste) and selling the images for a lot of money. He raised a fist to strike me, so I grabbed his wrist, twisted it, and jammed my thumb into the pressure point at the base of his index finger. His eyes went wide with pain. I calmly told him we were leaving and released his arm. The man slunk back into the crowd.

Somehow, we both managed to stay relatively healthy, although each of us suffered through the occasional intestinal distress or conjunctivitis. Pretty much every day my main meal consisted of chicken tikka masala. It was either that or curry, morning, noon, and night. I'm pretty sure I reeked of Indian spices for months after returning home.

Toward the end of August, we were thinking we had gathered pretty much everything we needed for our assignments. The work was getting more difficult and riskier, as word had spread of the Americans taking pictures of the casteless "beggars." There were more angry confrontations on the crowded streets. Kartik and Kamala were showing signs of nervousness whenever we hung around their home too long. Earlier that week a popular Army general was assassinated by who the newspapers described as "fair-skinned foreigners." While taking pictures from the Howrah Bridge, Joanna was detained by policemen who interrogated her about whom she was really working for. All a clear signal that perhaps it was time to cut bait.

There was only one last thing I really wanted to film: the annual Shravani Mela, a Hindu pilgrimage to Tarakeswar and the Temple of Shiva. We left the hotel one morning before dawn, and as the light broke as we reached the little village, we were astounded by the scene before us. Over a hundred thousand religious pilgrims, many of whom had traveled there on foot carrying water from the Ganges River to pour over the statue of Shiva, took up every square inch of space as far as the eye could see. Moving among the crowd, we were relieved to find the people friendly and accommodating, obviously focused on their own traditions and worshipful bliss. In keeping with custom, Jo and I took off our shoes and walked barefoot with the throng through the mud and broken shards of clay pots. The air was so thick with incense I felt dizzy. We watched goats being sacrificed, priests demanding *puja* (money) in return for their prayers, women throwing themselves down onto the muddy streets in religious fervor. It was one of the most glorious, baffling, fascinating scenes I've ever witnessed.

Two days later came the knock on my door and the warning that we were about to be arrested. I never found out if it was because someone finally checked on our permits, or lack thereof, or if our presence in the city had simply set off alarms. Regardless, Jo and I packed quickly, and at 4:00 a.m. Sri drove us and the gear to a smaller, regional airport, rather than the international airport, to avoid attention. Between us and the luggage, the cargo plane was nearly full.

Before climbing up the departure stairs, Jo and I gave Sri a considerable amount of money to set up a scholarship fund for the Singh children. Back then there were no public schools, only private. He promised to give the bankbook only to Kamala for her safekeeping, as Kartik was known to gamble and drink a bit on occasion. Having spent the past month every day with Sri, we had absolutely no doubt about his honesty and integrity. It was a tearful goodbye for us all.

The flight to the southern tip of India was long and bumpy. We hung out in beautiful Bangalore for a week, cleaning the gear, making notes about the material we had gathered, and decompressing from the humidity, heat, squalor, and crush of Calcutta. When we finally decided the coast was clear, we took a flight back to Europe via Bombay, and then home.

It took me five years to fall back in love with Indian cuisine.

CHAPTER 12

BACK OF BEYOND

There are still places on this earth without phones and electricity, without televisions and social media and highways and shopping malls and condominium complexes and Kardashians. Thank God.

But not many.

The GAZ-66 four-wheel-drive truck lumbered over the uneven ground at a steady pace of three miles an hour. We'd long ago left anything resembling an actual road and were now climbing higher into the Tian Shan mountains along a trail we were forging ourselves. The truck's enormous five-foot-tall knobby tires ate up boulders and muddy streams and even small trees without hesitation. Inside the GAZ, originally built to haul Soviet troops into the nearly impenetrable wildernesses of northern Russia and Siberia, I clung to whatever I could as the vehicle lurched side to side. The food stores in the kitchen area of the spacious converted interior were all secured. The blankets on the four bunk beds were tucked in as tight as a trampoline. But the seat I sat in had loose bolts holding it to the floor, so the long journey up and down the many mountains was an endless carnival ride.

Up front, the driver and guide, Bakhtiar, wrestled the big steering wheel, constantly upshifting and downshifting the 115 hp V8, which was underpowered but made up for it in torque. I'd hired him and his truck days ago at a ski resort that was closed for the summer to take us where few, if any, Westerners had ever been. In Kipling's words, the Back of Beyond.

The Tian Shan is a sparsely populated range in Central Asia that stretches along the borders of Kazakhstan, Kyrgyzstan, Uzbekistan, Tajikistan, and China. The name loosely translates to "Mountains of Heaven," which is an apt description. They are very tall. They are very rugged. And they are very, very beautiful.

A few days into the trip, we crested a rise and looked out on a vast high-altitude steppe next to a large lake. White yurts in the distance looked like wildflowers. We could see horsemen moving among their herds. There were no roads, electric lines, or buildings visible from horizon to horizon. The sun was sliding down in the sky like a pat of butter on a hot skillet, warning of only a few more hours of daylight.

As we wobbled further onto the semi-flat land, one of the nomads rode up. Bakhtiar stopped the GAZ and got out. Fortunately, the man knew some Russian. Bakhtiar explained who we were and why we were there. The man jumped on his horse and rode away.

"He says he will find the mayor," the guide explained.

We drove a little further into the valley and parked near the shore of the lake. Both of us were bruised and weary from days of bushwhacking through the wilderness. It seemed like only moments before the horseman returned on his small, spirited buckskin.

"The mayor has requested you join him for a feast this evening, to celebrate your presence," Bakhtiar translated.

That sounded lovely.

As the golden light began to fade, I shot as much footage as possible before our scheduled soiree. Women washing laundry at the edge of the lake while their colorfully dressed children played nearby. Large herds of horses wandering through the grassy fields, followed by one or two riders who looked so comfortable it seemed as though they were born on horseback.

In the days to come, I filmed the daily lives of these pastoral people. Women working inside their yurts, making tea, cooking dinner, playing with their children. A young boy, sitting on the ground on his saddle, repairing leather tack, harnesses, halters, and cinches that appeared to be a hundred years old, supple and worn and beautiful. I convinced one of the nomads to let me ride along as they worked their herd, and the pony he gave me was a head-tossing, sidestepping, independent-minded stick of dynamite, and I adored him. I have a sneaky suspicion the other riders were waiting for the horse to toss me off, and it's a badge of personal pride that he did not succeed.

One afternoon we heard a commotion. A group of men on horses were playing an exciting game called *kokpar*, a combination of polo, rugby, and keep-away. The sport originated with Genghis Khan's thirteenth-century warriors, for whom proficiency in horsemanship was the most important quality. In lieu of a football, the riders compete in violent scrums to grab and maintain control of a headless goat carcass. It is a fierce and fast and absolutely thrilling game. The riders, often at full charge, must lean almost completely off the back of their horse to grab the goat off the ground and then fend off the opposition, who are desperately struggling to wrest it away before he can fling it into his goal.

But make no mistake: the real athletes are the horses themselves. As small as polo ponies but as tough as NFL linebackers, these creatures were bred and raised to excel at what, in effect, is the national sport of many Central Asian nations. Unfortunately, the mayor forbade me from taking part, despite my pleas. I'm sure he didn't want to be known as the guy who allowed one of the only foreigners ever to visit the steppe to be killed on the field of play.

Only recently have the "Stans"—Kazakhstan, Kyrgyzstan, Tajikistan, and Uzbekistan—begun restoring their cultural identities after decades of Russification. Joseph Stalin was not the first Russian leader to institute such policies, but he was by far the most brutal. Beginning in the 1930s, he outlawed the teaching of regional languages and established Russian as the USSR's lingua franca. He forcibly deported native Russians to the Stans and sent tens of thousands of those countries' people to Siberia, with the goal of spreading the population of native Russian speakers from one end of the Soviet Union to the other. But, somehow, the people of the Back of Beyond managed to preserve much of their cultural identities.

Just before the sun dipped below the edge of the lake, the horseman on his little buckskin rode up and told Bakhtiar the mayor was ready for his photograph, which surprised me a bit, considering we hadn't requested one, but, OK, happy to do so.

We walked over to where the mayor sat outside his yurt, dressed in his very best suit, wearing the traditional *tubeteika* hat, and perched on a horse adorned with an ornamental leather breast collar. Holding onto the lead line was the mayor's unsmiling wife, resplendent in a bright-blue flowered dress with a matching headscarf. In the mayor's hand was a beautifully made riding crop, used for urging his horse to go faster. More than anything else, those small whips had become a symbol for his people that signified progress forward while maintaining a firm grip on the past. I still have the one given to me by the people of that valley before we left.

I clicked off a few photos of the proud husband and wife. The mayor laughed and announced, in effect, "Let's get this party started!"

Large tables had been set out in the open. Bakhtiar and I were seated at the head of one, the mayor at the other. We were given a glass of *kumis*—a bitter but interesting drink made from fermented mare's milk—for the initial toast to the visitors from America. Then the bottles of vodka were produced, and the drinks flowed. Large plates of roasted potatoes, trays of steamed vegetables, and slabs of delicious mutton were placed before us. After days of living on canned soup, protein bars, and nuts, I tucked in as if I were starving to death. At one point I was handed a well-cooked lamb's ear, which wasn't exactly appealing. But Bakhtiar explained it was an honor to receive that particular part of the animal. So I ate it.

Had I taken a bite out of the mayor's saddle, I'm not sure I would have noticed much difference in texture or taste.

After a few hours of gorging ourselves and drinking too much vodka, we stood to take our leave. It was probably around eight or nine o'clock. The mayor looked perplexed and said something to Bakhtiar, who turned to me with regret. "I'm sorry to tell you this, but the word has spread about the esteemed visitors, and the other mayors in the valley are awaiting your presence at their dinners to honor you."

The *other* mayors? "How many?"

Bakhtiar relayed the question to the mayor. "Four," he replied. "Maybe more."

We spent the better part of the rest of the night wandering from camp to camp, eating, drinking, and being entertained by song and story. We barely managed to stumble back to the GAZ just before sunrise and were likely already unconscious before our faces hit the pillows.

The hangover was sublime.

CHAPTER 13

THE WILD LIFE

"Let's see what the papers say this morning," the tall, bearded man said in his singsong Australian accent. He and I began to slowly walk around our camp in the Namib Desert, looking closely at the sandy ground for signs of the prior evening's activities. He pointed at some long scratches in the dirt. "Porcupine," he declared. "See where they drag their tails? Looks like a couple of them." Further on we spotted marks that resembled stitches in the silt, left by a hopping bird of some kind. A Cape fox family and a jackal had also come by, per usual, looking for any scraps of food.

To call the man next to me a legend is as obvious a statement as saying the sky is blue. Des Bartlett and his equally talented wife, Jen, were among the most famous wildlife filmmakers in the world for decades. Their work appeared on National Geographic in the United States and Anglia's *Survival* in Great Britain and pretty much everywhere else. One of their many films was the Emmy Award–winning *Flight of the Snow Geese*, an astounding piece of filmmaking for which Jen and Des tracked a flock of migrating birds almost 2,500 miles from the Hudson Bay to the Mississippi Delta. The film is most memorable because of the extreme close-ups the couple was able to make of the birds in actual flight, necks stretched out, wings languidly flapping, giving viewers the feeling of being among the geese as members of the skein. They accomplished that never-before-seen footage by filming from the back of a moving station wagon. Ordinarily, the birds would scatter and flee a motorized contraption, but Jen and Des had raised fourteen orphaned snow geese they met during four months of isolation in the birds' Arctic breeding grounds. The young birds imprinted on the humans and considered them their parents. Through patience and practice the couple was able to familiarize the birds with the noise and movement of the car. Shot from a low perspective with a wide-angle lens, the results are magical.

I first met Jen and Des through their daughter, Julie. I'd already spent many months in Africa over the years, working on various documentaries, and was casting about for another project when Julie mentioned the upcoming elections in South West Africa (now Namibia) and the controversies surrounding the actions of the United Nations peacekeeping force stationed there. Reports of rapes, brutality, and political favoritism were casting a dim light on the democratization of Africa's last colony. I'd found the subject of my next film.

Since 1915, South West Africa had been a territory under the administration of South Africa, with which it shared a border. Other neighboring countries were Angola, Botswana, and Zambia. Before 1915, South West Africa was a German colony, but after World War I the League of Nations mandated that the defeated nation relinquish it to South Africa's control. When the United Nations declared that mandate abolished in 1966, South Africa turned a deaf ear, perhaps because South West Africa had some of the largest diamond deposits in the world. The Skeleton Coast, called that in part because of all the shipwrecks offshore and bones of hapless survivors onshore, is one of De Beers's most profitable mining sites, where a large percentage of the company's $1.5 billion-valued harvest of precious stones are gathered each year. On some stretches of heavily guarded beaches, diamonds can reportedly be seen lying on the sand, glinting in the sun. Outsiders are not allowed.

After South Africa rejected international demands to free South West Africa, a bloody bush war, one of car bombs and sniper attacks and farm burnings, eventually broke out between the governing authority, now deemed illegal by pretty much every nation, and the South West Africa People's Organization (SWAPO). By the time the UN called for monitored elections in 1990, the fight was still waging.

About a month after that discussion with Julie Bruton, PBS's *Frontline* accepted my proposal, and I was on a plane to Johannesburg with soundman and guide Jim Bruton, Julie's now-former husband. We traveled around northern Namibia for weeks, interviewing dozens of officials and regular folk, filming the wreckage of the war, the UN monitors at work, and, ultimately, the elections themselves. Unfortunately, about the time we wrapped up production, I got word *Frontline* was dropping our deal. With Nelson Mandela's just being released from twenty-seven years in a South African prison, *Frontline* was preparing to air a documentary about his extraordinary life, and, in the words of the producer who called me, "There's only room for one program about Africa a year."

I had a case full of exposed film and audio recordings and a helluva story of corruption and resilience and triumph. I was also out tens of thousands of dollars, some of which was contributed by my friend and coinvestor Jack Bacot and my coproducer, Robert Green. Despite our disappointment, we eventually finished the film. *Namibia: The Last Colony* earned some prestigious awards and aired on a handful of PBS stations. The best thing to come out of the experience was the beginning of a friendship with Jen and Des Bartlett. What was to be a few days' stay with them after I finished filming my documentary stretched into weeks.

Des parceled out words slowly, as if he were dealing cards, but when he did speak, you paid attention. Jen, on the other hand, was a cheerful conversationalist, every bit as knowledgeable about wildlife and the natural world as her husband. She had made it to the second round at Wimbledon in 1956 before abandoning her tennis career to marry Des two months later. Shortly after the wedding, he handed her a camera and said, "Well, get with it!" Her gorgeous photographs graced many a page in multiple issues of the *National Geographic* magazine over the years.

Life at our desert camp, which the Bartletts called "Auses" (local for "oasis"), took place in near slow motion. Nature sets its own pace. It will not be hurried. We rose at dawn; habitually scanned the ground for the signs of nocturnal animal behavior Des referred to as "reading the morning papers"; and had a cup of tea (despite my preference for coffee), an orange, and a bowl of Jen's homemade muesli before starting the day's work. Lunch was a high-calorie sandwich of dark German bread, avocado, tomato, and sprouts as Mrs. Chat, a little bird who had adopted us, scolded anyone who didn't throw her bits of cheese quickly enough. Dinner was usually salad; fish we caught in the roaring, frigid southern Atlantic; and a delicious vegetarian concoction whipped up by Jen or Julie; or I'd occasionally make omelets for everyone. A small, precious portion of Old Brown sherry by the fire as we listened to the BBC on a shortwave radio capped off the day. Much of the time was taken up with the basics of survival in the vast wilderness, hundreds of miles from the nearest town. There was cleaning to be done and repairs to be made on the film cameras, maintenance of the Land Rover and Ford F-250 truck and microlight airplanes, and copious notetaking of what footage was shot the previous day.

Jen and Des worked in 16 mm film, so it was imperative that every frame was accounted for—with detailed notes about the subject animals, what happened, time of day, angle of the sun, weather conditions, and direction of movement—

because we couldn't replay what we'd shot as one would with video.

For example, these are some of my notes from July 3:

> 9:30am—Spider web glistening with dew, water in oasis sparkles behind it. Female Gemsbok arrives from right dune w/2 young—one very young w/3 inch horns and another w/ 10 inchers. They emerge from behind dune and she leads way down slipface [sic]. The two follow, pan from her to them. Next shot is her ½ way down. They run past her and [camera] follows them. Family walks to Salvadora bush and begins feeding. Various shots. Youngster goes to Nara [a fruiting plant] first. They all move to Nara and feed. Various shots. One shot is of female eating Nara facing camera. At one point female lunges at oldest youth behind Nara to chase him farther away. Various of reactions. Shot of youths standing together. Youngest reaches back and nibbles older's tail. He leaves. Cam stays on baby. Large male appears. Shot of him walking past Nara, tilt to baby looking on. Male has long scar on left shoulder. Female lunges at him—but partially screened by bush. Last shot is of older youth trying to suckle—partially screened. Mother walks away from him.

Wildlife films are built on a series of images and angles that are almost never shot at the same exact moment, so knowing whether the editor has a complete sequence that can authentically convey a single event is imperative. In a finished film, a cheetah chasing down an antelope calf might actually consist of separate moments that happened over the course of weeks, if not months, and then are edited together to create a seamless movie sequence. Cheetah stalks something through the brush. Antelope startles, looking around. Francolin birds squawk in alarm. Cheetah bolts. Antelope bolts. Chase ensues. A blur of running legs. Other animals looking on. Cheetah eventually pulls down (or fails to pull down) antelope. You get the picture.

The best days I can remember were either when Des and I took to the air in one of the two microlight airplanes they used—called "Drifters"—to get aerials of animals or when I got to station myself in the blind hidden in the rocks next to the water hole. The blind was made of beige canvas, not much bigger than a porta-potty and stiflingly hot when the sun was up. Whoever was manning the cameras there on any given day had to leave before sunrise to be in place well before the first animals arrived. But from its small openings, you could witness almost every kind of animal behavior.

The water hole sometimes resembled the Mos Eisley Cantina scene from *Star Wars: A New Hope*. All kinds of creatures gathered there for a drink. Most had traveled for miles across arid lands for that quenching slurp.

One morning I rose early and used the dim light from the nearly full moon to keep to the path Des had shown me. The desert was silent and chilly. Not even the birds were awake yet. Eventually, I could smell the oasis before I even reached the shale cliffs that stretched down to the water on one side. The trickiest part was climbing down to the blind in the dark without loosening any rocks or tumbling down myself, but once inside I loaded the Arriflex camera by feel, set it and the Nikon still camera on their tripods, and sat back against the scratchy rock, closed my eyes, and waited.

I learned from the Bartletts that the most important tool in wildlife photography is patience. Animals aren't paid performers—they live their lives on their own terms, in their own time. The second most important tool is anticipation. Thousands of tourists return home from safari each year with wonderful collections of butt pictures. The Cape buffalo walking away. The lion pride in retreat. The north side of a southbound rhino. Shooting motion picture film is even more difficult. To create a moment of authentic behavior, one must start rolling before the action begins. That takes instinct, knowledge, and a great deal of luck.

When the sun broke above the horizon, the temperature in the blind began to rapidly climb. I leaned forward and scanned the area around the water hole. Already, a handful of birds had descended on the shore and in the bushes next to it, raising a cacophony with their greetings and squabbles. A jackal slunk down to the edge, casting about furtive looks between sips. I found myself watching an ellipsis of Camponotus ants marching across the rock where I sat. The hours passed without anything of note happening, yet I was as happy as I could possibly be, sitting there in the stifling heat. Being an unobtrusive witness, watching the world as it has existed for millennia, is as close to Zen-like meditation as I've ever been able to achieve.

Memory is a funny thing. I've told this next story so many times over the years that I was stunned when Jen, while fact-checking this chapter, explained the scene I describe below could not have happened where I thought it did, at the oasis near our camp. She said, in fact, that no elephants had ventured close to Auses the entire year I was with the Bartletts. So the event I witnessed had to have happened elsewhere. In this instance my journal was no help—between my almost illegible scribbles and an occasional missing date, the details were unclear. I dug into a box of photographic slides from my time in Namibia to try to solve the mystery, and Jen's suspicions were confirmed—the Day of the Elephants happened at a different water hole, near Etosha National Park. Regardless of the confusion, it was a remarkable thing to see.

My photographs show a broad, flat, rocky plain with a variety of spindly Tamarisk trees and hardy bushes surrounding a fairly large oasis. In one I'm pictured with the Arriflex on a tripod, crouched behind some vegetation near the edge of the water. The leather jacket I'm wearing tells me it was probably taken in the early morning, before the sun erased the chill from the air.

I remember watching a few animals wandering around when suddenly something shifted in the ether. There was movement to my right. I triggered the Arri and panned in that direction just as a large, dark form emerged from behind the brush: an adult elephant. She peered around, her ears fanned wide, her trunk testing the air for threats. Apparently satisfied, she trumpeted a short signal, and a group of smaller elephants quickly joined her. The herd proceeded to make their way to the water's edge and begin drinking.

Anthropomorphism is a bad word in the world of nature filmmaking. Attributing human characteristics and motives to animals is generally frowned upon as simplistic and unscientific, yet these days it's almost impossible for documentary makers to hold an audience without an emotional story arc focusing on attractive or cutely strange-looking animals. Ugly generally doesn't sell. Nature films have become steadily more Disneyfied, with dramatic conflicts and human names for the various "characters." The dilemma for filmmakers is that without an appreciative audience, there would be no money to produce these movies, outside of dry, academic studies. And they do serve an important service, reminding humans that we are part of a larger ecosystem that must be honored and protected.

That said, it's undeniable animals do, on occasion, exhibit behaviors that resemble our own, perhaps because we, too, are animals.

As the elephants splashed around in the oasis, I changed the film magazine and rolled off some more shots with the Arri and the Nikon. Then the matriarch (I'd learned from Des that bull elephants are usually off on their own except in mat-ing season) gave another signal, and the herd trudged out of the water and up onto shore.

The elephants lined up, single file, and walked around the far side of the oasis to a large, blackish-gray shape lying on the ground. Southern Africa at the time was enduring an anthrax outbreak, and, although less devastated by the deadly bacteria than her neighbors, Namibia was not immune. It can be assumed that's likely what killed this elephant because he still bore his magnificent tusks, which, had he been a victim of poaching—thankfully rare in Namibia—would have already been removed with a chain saw.

As I watched through the Arri's viewfinder, the female moved slowly up to the carcass, draped her trunk over the back, and stood motionless for what seemed like two or three minutes before moving on. Then, one by one, her children followed suit. When the last elephant stepped away, the family walked into the brush and out of my sight.

Anthropomorphic conclusion or not on my part, there isn't an animal behaviorist in the world who could ever convince me those elephants weren't paying their last respects. There was no way of knowing if this was the herd's father, or if these wonderful animals were just saying goodbye to a fallen friend. But if you don't believe animals are capable of emotion, you've never looked into the eyes of a loyal dog.

With no mechanics within hundreds of miles, having some ability with a wrench comes in handy. The Bartletts were having problems with both of the Drifter's engines, so Des and I spent days working on them and finally narrowed the issues down to the carburetors and distributors. The fine silt constantly blowing in the desert wind wreaked havoc on sensitive motor parts. My notes from June 23 include a sketch of the ignition coils so that I could replace everything as it should be.

After stripping and cleaning both carbs, we got Jen's Drifter 2 running somewhat raggedly, but Drifter 1 purred like a kitten. Des took her up to about five hundred feet, and she flew beautifully...until the engine suddenly cut out completely. He coasted her down to a graceful landing (one of the great things about microlights—they're basically gliders with motors). I made a few more adjustments, and he went up again. The Drifter flew fine for a few moments and then, again, died. Des landed safely, but we were all frustrated. My notes in the journals indicated I suspected the pistons were seizing. We'd need a more expert mechanic than me, so we eventually called a friend of the Bartletts, Wolfgang Rapp, to come help. He was able to diagnose the problem as a ball valve in the fuel line.

Finally, on the twenty-eighth, we were able to get both Drifters up and flying perfectly. That meant the long-delayed trip up north to film elephants was back on schedule. We all celebrated that evening with Old Brown, grapes, and cheese. Mrs. Chat, the camp mascot, was delighted.

One of the methods filmmakers use to get intimate peeks into the lives of wild animals is to capture them, familiarize them with human presence, and then film them up close as they go about their daily activities. That's as hard as it sounds. The Bartletts had permission to do so with small- to medium-sized animals and reptiles. Snakes were easy; mammals less so. Prime example: the Porky Rodeo Roundup.

One morning, I was following some porcupine tracks away from camp. The wind hadn't yet picked up, so the scat was clearly visible. These particular porcupines, native to southern Africa, are very large, weighing up to fifty pounds, with extremely long quills. Contrary to popular myth, porcupines can't throw their quills, but they are adept at quickly swinging their body around to painfully imbed their built-in spears into whatever creature is trying to make them a snack. They're not the smartest of creatures, but they haven't survived all this time in one of the most formidable environments by being pushovers either. Des explained that, like most species of rodents, taming them would be relatively easy once we had them in a fenced-off area. But first we had to catch them.

As I approached a Nara bush, I saw a plume of sand thrown in the air. The object of my search was still there, digging at the base of the bush to get at the succulent roots. I ran back to camp and told Des. He and I grabbed a couple of cameras and hurried back. As Des began rolling film, the porcupine was silhouetted against the rising sun. It was a magnificent scene. We quietly moved around to the other side. The porky's head was deep inside a hole he'd dug, oblivious of our presence. Soon, Jim Bruton joined us. Des wanted a different lens and asked us to keep an eye on the porcupine. "If he starts to leave," he told us, "run at him to scare him back into the hole."

Just as Des and Jen returned with more camera gear, the porcupine lifted his head up, spotted us, and made a break for it. "Run like hell!" Des shouted.

I took off around the dune and actually caught up with him, but those little porky legs propelled him like a train. I tried to scare him as I ran alongside to herd him back toward the others, but he angled in my direction, sideways, with quills extended. I had to jump away. I could hear Jim running behind us, laughing so hard he could barely keep up. I had my hat in my hand with arms extended to try to turn the animal. He ignored me and kept plugging along.

Jim and I chased that damn thing for what felt like half a mile, making ridiculous lion noises and laughing and shouting. Finally, all three of us ran out of steam. The porcupine retreated into a Tamarisk thicket to catch his breath. I sat there the rest of the day, eight feet away from the porky, while the Bartletts and Jim returned to camp to build a pen. Des was very excited at the prospect of finally catching and taming a porcupine after eight years of trying. He decided not to use a net for fear of damaging the animal's quills, so he, Julie, Jen, and Jim returned with some large plywood boards and some shade fabric to corral the prickly porky.

Once the others were in position and ready, I climbed into the Tamarisk from the opposite side to flush him out. At first he resisted, just hissing and lunging at me. Then he bolted, right into the trap.

They had him! But only for a moment. He threw his weight into the fabric and managed to push his way underneath.

Once again, it was a footrace with a Rodent of Unusual Size, to borrow from William Goldman's *The Princess Bride*. I kicked off my sandals in order to run faster and quickly regretted having done so when we reached some sharp-edged schist. As the porky, with me in close pursuit, reached the top of the rocky ledge, Jim came huffing and puffing up the other side. We had him trapped again. The only escape was through one of us. He simply stopped and glared with his little beady eyes, breathing heavily.

The rest of our team arrived around four-thirty in the afternoon. I suggested we lay out the shade netting and prompt the porky to move on top of it, then simply lift it off its feet, but Des vetoed that out of concern for the porcupine's safety. Instead, he had us all positioned with the large plywood boards again. At his signal, I began walking slowly forward with my board. The porky immediately slammed all his weight back into me and took off down the hill. Julie pinned him for a moment, but he threw her aside and kept going. Like an NFL running back, the rodent feinted around Des and disappeared from sight.

The dirty, sweaty, disappointed kidnappers all sat down and had a good laugh. We never did catch a porcupine. A few weeks later I turned a corner around a sand dune, and there stood the big porky, staring at me calmly as he munched on a dry twig, unperturbed and unconcerned. After all, he'd handled these human things before.

As I said, life in the desert had its own pace. Or perhaps it was set by Des's slow, methodical, graceful way of doing things. He was quiet, gentle, observant, and supremely thoughtful. I learned a great deal from just watching him, and a great deal more from our talks.

I'd taken it upon myself to find the den of a beautiful Cape fox who was frequenting our campsite at night. We spotted her every once in a while, moving silently through our midst just outside the flickering light of the campfire. My hope was to position a remote camera inside her home to film her caring for her pups.

Every morning I wasn't in the blind or on repair duty I'd set out just after dawn, following her tracks in the sand. It was imperative to do so before the wind picked up and erased them, which typically happened at noon. Wearing just a pair of shorts with a canteen and small umbrella strapped around my waist, I'd walk for hours over the soft dunes and hard pack, enjoying the solitude. On one occasion I spotted a cheetah walking on the hard pack, watching me with mild interest (I was too big to be considered easy prey), and yet another morning I caught a rare daytime glimpse of a hyena. The umbrella, by the way, was not for protection against the rain—it was a defense against a possible animal attack. None of us ever carried a gun; in fact, we didn't even have one in camp. Instead, Des theorized, should an animal ever charge us, a rapidly opening umbrella pointed in their direction was a shocking enough development to change the mind of pretty much any wild animal. I'm glad I never had to test the theory on a charging lion.

Des did have a stun gun in the medical kit, but that wasn't for use as a weapon. Instead, a zap of high-voltage electricity immediately breaks down snake venom, so the Bartletts had it on hand should any of us get bitten by one of the poisonous adders, cobras, or asps that shared our desert home. Des once told me the story of how someone saved a man's life who'd suffered a viper strike by zapping him with a pair of jumper cables attached to the coil of his truck engine. Even though car batteries are only twelve volts, coils can produce up to forty thousand.

Day after day I'd go as far as I could until the fox tracks faded away, take note of the location relative to the familiar rocky hills in the distance, then return to camp. I'd get a little farther each time, until one day I finally reached a rocky escarpment full of nooks and crannies and tiny caves. I was certain this was the fox's home. But after describing it to Des, he said, in his wonderfully musical cadence, "Don, she'll never show you where her babies are, and she'll leave no tracks on rock. The only chance you'd have is to set up some night vision trail cameras to see where she goes in, and we don't have any." That was the end of my search for the fox den. But not the end of my walks in the desert.

Those failures notwithstanding, we did have some success in capturing and taming our subjects. Most notable was when an African fruit bat flew into our lives.

We were sitting around the fire after a long, hot day, sipping sherry and listening to "the Beeb," as Jen and Des called it—the BBC's Africa service—on shortwave radio, when a fluttering suddenly started up around our heads. We could hear and even feel the sharp peeps of echolocation he was using to map out the surroundings. A dark figure swooped in and out of the firelight before landing on our clothesline and hanging upside down. His face, as lovely as a collie's, turned to look at all of us before he winged away.

Bats are not native to that part of the desert. At least not willingly. But this guy was a victim of what the locals call the "East Wind," when the prevailing winds occasionally shift from coming off the Atlantic Ocean to blowing in from the mainland. When that happened, we'd see colorful birds and butterflies in the otherwise drab landscape. Unfortunately, unless they could navigate their way back to the more hospitable climate of the interior, their little journey doomed them to a quick death.

The next night, at about the same time, it happened again. The bat fluttered in, settled on the clothesline and perused the scene. This time, he stayed a little longer before flying away to some mysterious location. That's when Jen had an idea.

Before dark the following evening, I took a few of our precious grapes, peeled them, and attached them to the cord. Then we sat, enjoying our tiny daily dram of Old Brown, and waited. He didn't keep us long.

The bat wheeled around our heads twice and landed on the line. Immediately, he turned his attention to the first grape. Crawling along claw over claw he approached it, took one sniff, then began munching happily. He languidly moved from one grape to the next, and when they were all gone, he flapped his huge wings and was gone.

It took all of two more nights before I literally had him eating out of my hand. I'll never forget his beautiful large eyes and the incredible softness of his wings. He allowed me to stroke his back as he ate and never once tried to bite me. That bat became a regular nightly visitor for weeks. Des even made a short film about him with his and Jen's grandson Tarl. Then all of a sudden he stopped coming. The prevailing winds had changed back to normal. I'd like to think he took the opportunity to fly back home to his family, with many a story to tell them.

Our camp at Auses was situated in the Skeleton Coast National Park, which has very restricted access and only one road in or out, which ran along the coast. Tourists were forbidden unless they had the correct permits and were accompanied by one of a handful of licensed tour guides. Namibia is fiercely antipoaching, with standing shoot-to-kill orders for their game officers. As a result, the wildlife population of the northwest part of the country is among the healthiest and most protected in the world.

That remoteness is a paradise for nature filmmakers, but it also makes for a difficult existence. We were hundreds of miles away from the nearest town. Everything we ate, drank, and depended upon had to be hauled in. There were no land-lines, no cell phones, no communication of any kind from the desert camp. In the event of an emergency, we would have to travel overland to the ranger station at Möwe Bay, where we then radioed an operator in Walvis Bay, over three hundred miles away, to be connected to a phone line.

One day we had loaded up the two vehicles, an old Land Rover and a Ford F-250, with aluminum pipes for an elevated blind we planned to build in the gravel plains north of camp. The trip there was a tricky one. Hauling that much weight overland without roads required stopping every now and then to let air out of the tires in order to cross the soft sandy stretches, then refilling them on the other side, only to repeat the process at the next obstacle.

I was driving the Ford. Des had wanted me to get a little practice with it going through the deep sand. As he was coaching me how to disengage the transmission from low gear by first putting it into reverse, the heavily laden truck lurched forward and started plowing through the sand. Then there was an enormous *bang!* The Ford stopped dead in its tracks.

I climbed out and shimmied underneath it. I immediately saw the differential shaft had snapped at its universal joint. The truck was going nowhere. I climbed out and told Des the bad news. He couldn't hide his disappointment.

It was my fault, I was certain, but Des waved off my apologies and, in his inimitably calm fashion, sat down to think of what to do.

"Can we get a replacement in Swakop?" I asked, using the slang name for Namibia's closest city, Swakopmund, a full day's drive away.

He shook his head. "Not for a Ford, I don't think, Don. They'd have to ship one in from Jo-burg. That'll take time."

"Well, then, I think it can be fixed," I told him. "It was a clean break where the joint meets the solid steel shaft. A good welder should be able to do it."

"But will it be able to stand the strain?"

I wasn't sure. And I told him. But it was worth a try. We needed the Ford.

Everyone else climbed into the Landy and returned to camp while I set about removing the differential. It took me a bit of time, but finally I got the shaft off and carried it back to Auses.

Later that afternoon, Jim and I loaded up the empty gas and water cans into the Land Rover and headed out on the fifty-mile-long drive to Terrace Bay, which had the closest repair shop. Unfortunately, the welding equipment there was broken. As we contemplated making an even longer drive down the coast to the larger city of Swakopmund, a couple of conservationists on their way into the wilderness offered to help. One of them, Jan Grobler, assured us he knew how to weld. It just so happened there was a working machine back at Möwe Bay, so we headed back there.

It was crucial that the metal shaft be perfectly plumb, otherwise the oscillations when the engine was running would tear it apart. As Jan finished the repairs, I took the opportunity to take a long, hot bath and make a radio call to Sara James, my wife at the time. Jim and I filled up the Landy with supplies and, under the light of the half-moon, eventually found our way back to camp.

The following morning, Des and I journeyed out to the disabled Ford, and I reinstalled the shaft, holding my breath the entire time.

When I was done, Des climbed in and started it up as I stood by, watching with dread. Without a word, he put it in gear and began easing it forward. There was no loud shriek, no bang. So far so good. He increased the speed. The Ford kept moving. I stretched out on the ground to look underneath. The shaft was turning smoothly without a wobble. The repair was holding.

"Well done, Don!" Des declared. I felt as though I'd just won the Oscar.

We eventually made it to the gravel plains and beyond, to the Hoanib River, where we filmed elephants, including the legendary Hoarusib bull, a gigantic male elephant that traveled unbelievable distances across the Namib Desert. Jen and Des had seen him before, closer to camp. I had a memorable encounter with the giant when he ambled within twenty feet of me, filming from the safety of the Ford, before giving his massive head a warning shake in my direction that said, "Stay clear, little person." The ground literally shook as he walked by.

My relatively brief time with Jen and Des in Namibia had some of the happiest, most fascinating days of my life. I'm forever grateful for their hospitality and how generous they were with their knowledge. I would see them now and then through the years whenever they came back to the US, and our reunions were always filled with laughter and stories. One of the most difficult decisions I ever made was to not become a wildlife filmmaker myself. Des had arranged for me to meet the good people at Anglia Television on my way back to the States to see if they'd be interested in any of my ideas for nature films, but ultimately I realized that not only would a life in the wild all by myself be lonely; it would be akin to my becoming Peter Pan, the boy who wouldn't grow up. I had too many other things I wanted to accomplish.

When I got the call in the fall of 2009 that Des had passed away after suffering a stroke, it was a punch to my stomach. He was more than a mentor to me. He was a friend I deeply loved and admired. I can't remember him without being reminded of a John Muir quote about how most of us have nothing more than a passing relationship to the world, on it but not in it Well, Des Bartlett was an exception to that. He was definitely in the world, and his contributions to the understanding of it are priceless.

Jen and I have remained in touch to this day.

CHAPTER 14

THE OCTOPUS'S GARDEN

We were taking a break from the desert at Jen and Des Bartlett's seaside cabin at Möwe Bay in Namibia to make repairs, do laundry, and catch enough fish to feed us for a few weeks. My bucket was already full of what I'd hauled in from the surf that morning, so I was wandering around the tidal pools along the shore to see what creatures were trapped in them. That's when I spotted a long, tentacled arm feeling around the lava rocks. It was an octopus, pinkish brown, about a foot long, not counting its arms. When he noticed me he quickly jerked back into the water, but I could still see him watching me with the two eyes on top of his head.

I kneeled down to study him closer. He leaned upward to do the same to me.

After a few moments he reached out tentatively with one of his tentacles and let it rest on the rocky surface next to my foot. I slowly moved my hand forward until we touched. Instead of yanking his tentacle away, he wrapped the tip around one of my fingers. I could feel the strength of his suction cups. The skin around them was as smooth as glass.

He lifted his head out of the water. I rummaged around in the bucket with my other hand and pulled out one of the small baitfish, holding it up for him to see. Without hesitation, the octopus wrapped a tentacle around it, took it out of my grasp, and slid down deeper into the tidal pool and under a ledge where I could no longer see him.

Minutes later, he was back. I gave him another fish. He submerged to eat it.

I returned to that spot a few times that day and the next. I began to think he was waiting for me to appear. He would lift his head out of the water each time I approached. When he wasn't eating the fish I'd brought him, he would crawl completely out of the water and sit on my legs, playing around with anything shiny—buttons or my watch, about which he was especially fascinated. He gently explored the contours of my face and pulled on my hair, lifting himself up to look me in the face. There was an obvious intelligence in his eyes, a curiosity, and a fearlessness.

Eventually I came back with a film camera, thinking perhaps there was a little story to be told about life in the tidal pools. But my eight-armed friend was gone, swimming around the floor of the Atlantic, I hoped, and telling his friends about this human he'd tamed and taught to bring him lunch.

CHAPTER 15

THE IMPORTANCE OF MOVING WELL

There was one bus on Grenada, which seemed appropriate given there was also only one road. It circled the mountainous island like a headband holding back a shock of unruly green hair. There was no regular schedule. One simply stood by the side of the road and waved down the garishly painted bus as it approached.

Lugging a bag of fins, a snorkel, and a mask, I climbed aboard and settled into a seat that was more duct tape than original vinyl. Taking an afternoon off from working on a free-lance travel article for the *Richmond Times-Dispatch* (which began, "The birth pains of a new day come early on the sea. It peeks over the edge of the horizon like an infant peering over the rim of his crib."), I had a vague idea of where I was going to do some snorkeling, and, per the philosophy of life in the Caribbean, I wasn't in no hurry, *mon*.

The plan was to meet a local fellow named Arian I'd met the day prior who convinced me the best diving in the whole area could be found at a remote point on the island where few residents and fewer still tourists would venture. Two stops up from where I boarded, he, too, climbed on and plopped down on the seat next to me. He pulled a cold Carib beer out of his rucksack and handed it to me.

"It's nine in the morning," I replied.

"Naw, mon. You're on Grenada time now."

In the spirit of international cooperation, I popped the tab and enjoyed a morning brewski. The bus rumbled along, disgorging a passenger here and there on the way, gathering others. We talked about the world, movies, politics, and diving. Arian was intelligent and informed despite having left school in fifth grade to earn a living for his family. Every once in a while a rusting tank or military jeep peeked out from the thick brush, casualties of the humiliating 1983 invasion of Grenada by the US military, which ended a Cuban-backed communist coup d'état. After about fifteen minutes, Arian stood and said, "We here." We climbed down the stairs, and the bus departed in a cloud of black diesel smoke. I looked around. Jungle. More jungle. And a steep hill that meandered down to the sea.

"This way," my new friend said, pushing aside some lush branches to reveal what may have been an actual path. We carefully picked our way down, half-sliding, half falling, until we reached a miniscule patch of sandy beach no more than ten feet wide. Arian sat down, opened his ragged canvass bag, and pulled out a homemade diving mask constructed of bicycle tubing, glue, Velcro strap, and a flat piece of window glass. Next followed a speargun fashioned from a metal pipe, a clothespin, and rubber hose. He had no fins, and no snorkel.

I was sincerely embarrassed to don my expensive commercially manufactured mask, fins, and snorkel.

There are so many adjectives I could pick to describe the blue of the Caribbean we slipped into on the southernmost point of that tiny island: azure, turquoise, cobalt. Every one is accurate. And every one falls pathetically short as a representative of its stunning beauty.

We swam about fifty feet offshore, took a deep breath, and kicked down to the reef below. A frenetic rainbow of fish of every color wheeled around us, fearless and curious about the new intruders. By that time in my life, I had scuba dived in almost every popular site in the Western Hemisphere, but I'd never seen such a rich ecosystem. It was like being immersed in the vibrant screen saver that became popular on early high-definition computer monitors.

Out of the corner of my eye I saw Arian motion to me. I was close to needing to head to the surface for another breath of air, but I followed him even deeper to the coral bottom. There, he pointed at a clump of pinkish-orange sea urchins. He plucked two off the coral and swam to the surface.

I followed.

As we bobbed around in the gentle waves, Arian produced a knife and cracked open one of the creatures, handing it to me. He did the same with his own and demonstrated how to scoop out the yellow goop inside with his fingers and eat it.

Again, I followed. Unsure of what I was getting into. But I followed.

It was delicious. Sweet and eggy, unlike anything I'd ever tasted.

We spent the rest of the day diving down to the coral reef to explore, surfacing for a breath, then diving down again. Even without fins, Arian was as fast a swimmer as I was with them. I gathered a few branches of black coral to make into jewelry for friends (now a protected species, but fair game at the time). Late in the afternoon Arian speared a large dolphin-fish—not the mammal; it's known elsewhere as mahi-mahi—and signaled to me it was time to depart. As we stripped off our diving gear on the little beach, he explained he didn't want the fish to go bad before he could get home and grill it.

"Good fish," he said. "Very good. My wife will be happy."

We started the long climb up the hill to the road. The same bus that dropped us off earlier in the morning rounded the curve around 4:00 p.m. and opened its door for us to board. Arian and I made our way to the only open seats in the back. The passengers we shuffled by, many of whom apparently knew my diving companion, commented on his trophy while casting a curious eye in my direction. The locals sitting next to us were chatty and friendly. Americans, it turns out, were very welcome on their island after ending a violent period of political upheaval.

The return bus ride was longer than the original trip to the dive spot, as we had to wind our way back around the entire island. About halfway there my black coral began to smell. Badly. Like, really badly. The living organism surrounding the hard, shiny center was dying. Imagine a three-day-old fish left in the hot sun, and you get a tiny idea of the stench. People on the bus began commenting.

Arian just laughed.

"Yah mon," he declared loudly. "This is the way white people smell when they get wet!" He put his arm around my shoulders as the entire bus guffawed.

As we neared my stop, I thanked Arian for an unforgettable day, and he leaned in close. "Hey. Listen. You know what? I like you, mon. You move well."

"What, like, swim?"

He shook his head and motioned to the passengers around us on the bus. "Naw. You move well." Then I got it. He meant among other people, people not like me. A stranger in a strange land, comfortable nonetheless. It was, without a doubt, the greatest compliment I've ever received.

It also formed my philosophy on how to be a good journalist.

Set ego aside. Be a fellow human. Shed any attitude of superiority or condescension. Listen. Talk. Learn. Absorb. Taste unfamiliar local cuisines. And respect everyone for what they do with what they have.

Move well.

That could also explain why I've never been considered a "star." Over the decades I collected a few shelves full of the most prestigious awards for television journalists. But in many ways my broadcasting career was one of "almost." Almost Katie

Couric's replacement at the CBS News anchor desk. Almost a *60 Minutes* correspondent. Almost a *GMA* host. Almost a big deal. Instead, I was almost invisible, a journeyman reporter who got to cover most of the biggest stories of his time for the best news organizations on the planet but was ignored for the very biggest *jobs* by corporate executives.

And you know what? I'll take that deal. Every damn time.

CHAPTER 16

A HUMBLE SAINT

She moved more slowly than the morning sun creeping over the horizon. Her slippered feet shuffled along the bare wooden floor, making the softest of sounds, accompanied by the click of her cane every other step. When she reached me, the tiny woman raised her head to look me in the eye, then smiled. That unforgettable face, crinkled by millions of creases and eight decades of an amazing life, was still beautiful.

As a young woman, Anjezë Gonxhe Bojaxhiu was the prettiest girl in her Albanian village. She went on to devote her life to loving and caring for the poorest of the poor, often begging openly on the streets for food to feed the hungry. She braved leprosy and HIV/AIDS to comfort people ignored by the rest of the world. "A beautiful death," she wrote, "is for people who lived like animals to die like angels—loved and wanted."

Over the preceding year I'd written countless letters pleading with her people for an interview. The responses were always a very polite but very persistent no. So this visit was a last Hail Mary—traveling to the Missionaries of Charity in India to appeal to the great woman in person.

"Thank you for seeing me," I said. "As I told your staff, I'm making a documentary about the people of this great city, and I strongly believe it would be incomplete without including you. You're such an important, crucial part of this community."

The shriveled little hand that had held the sick, the dying, and the lost reached over to pat mine. "I have been interviewed thousands of times. I'm far more famous than I ever wanted to be, but it served a purpose, bringing attention to those in need. I have no desire to be on television again. But you may interview any of the other sisters who are willing."

With that, she turned and left, as slowly as she had arrived.

Twenty-five years later, that woman, who the world came to know as Mother Teresa, was canonized a saint by Pope Francis.

CHAPTER 17

THE EMPEROR'S PETS

Ethiopia's capital, Addis Ababa, in the late '80s. With a rare afternoon free, I decided to visit the palace of the former emperor Haile Selassie. Selassie is regarded by Rastafarians as a deity whose bloodline allegedly dated back to King Solomon and the Queen of Sheba. The man, originally known as Ras Tafari, was proclaimed emperor in 1930. One of the first actions of his forty-five-year reign was to establish the nation's first constitution and create a bicameral legislature. Despite his efforts to end feudalism, his government was often criticized for a lack of political freedom and a poor human rights record. A crippling famine in the early 1970s that killed an estimated 200,000 eventually led to a military coup. Selassie died while under house arrest, still believing he was emperor.

Across the street from the palace stood an enormous billboard erected by the existing communist government, featuring the profiles of Marx, Lenin, and Stalin. One of the locals had pointed it out to me the day before. "We call that Three Men with One Ear" he joked. Surprisingly, the gate to the palace was open, so I wandered inside the grounds, expecting to be stopped at any moment. There were no guards and few people around, but a very old, tiny man spotted me and waved.

When I reached him he introduced himself as the former emperor's butler. As he showed me around the place, he chatted about what life used to be like before Selassie died in 1975. "I'm the only one left," he said. "Well, except for them." He pointed to two large cheetahs lolling around on their backs, enjoying the sun. "Those were his favorite pets. My job is to take care of them now." Selassie had raised cheetahs from the early days of his reign. The man told me that these two were born shortly before he died. I did the math in my head—these animals had to be around fifteen years old, ancient by cheetah standards.

We walked over to the big cats. One stretched, stood, and slowly approached us. "Don't worry," the man said. "They're very friendly. But very old."

Like a house cat would, the cheetah bumped his head against my leg. I could hear him purring. As I reached down to pet him, he flopped onto his back again and enjoyed a good belly scratch. I noticed his paws looked more like a dog's. When I commented on that the former butler nodded. "Their feet are for running, not fighting. They kill by strangling their prey after they've tired them from the chase." The cat reached over and gave my arm a long lick. His rough tongue felt as though it was sanding the skin clean off.

"What do they like to eat now?" I asked.

The old man cackled. "Tourists!" he declared. I'm fairly certain he was joking.

CHAPTER 18

SOMETIMES YOU GET LUCKY

Dateline, Uganda. The brutal and bloody civil war had been raging since 1980 as followers of Idi Amin and the unpopular president Milton Obote battled for control of the beautiful nation once known as the Pearl of Africa. In 1986 I was traveling there with a small group of American journalists covering an emerging health crisis known locally as "the slimming disease." No one yet knew its cause, but thousands of Ugandans were dying from the mysterious sickness, and international researchers had been dispatched to try to understand why. It was the genesis of what eventually became known as the AIDS epidemic.

On the road to a remote research facility, we came upon one of many checkpoints manned by various rebel armies. It was in an area named the Luwero Triangle, where much of the killing and dying had happened. We had already passed rows of hundreds of human skulls roadside, mounted on sticks. Local farmers complained their cattle were constantly injuring their feet from walking on bone fragments. The actual number of Ugandans who died in the civil war is unknown but thought to be upward of half a million.

I was driving. Normally at such checkpoints we would flash our credentials or offer a contribution to the cause of a few bucks and be on our way. But this time the young soldier standing next to the barricade, dressed in a combination of army fatigues and a Mickey Mouse T-shirt, waved his rifle menacingly for us to get out of the car. Two child soldiers stood nearby, their weapons trained on the three foreigners who dared to travel through their territory.

"Who are you?" the young man asked. I figured him to be nine years old at most. His eyes were not friendly. The word *baleful* comes to mind.

"We're journalists. Press. You know, television," I replied, showing him my credentials.

He was unimpressed. Pointing his AK-47 directly at my face, he declared, "You are spies. I can shoot you."

At that moment I could see the gears turning in his head. I imagined he was wondering if my brains would look like those of all the other gunshot victims he'd seen in his young life. Or, on the other hand, if he'd get into trouble for killing these *mzungu*—white men.

It's been my experience that in situations like that there are a limited number of options: beg, bribe, or bluster. Considering the boy's age, I chose the latter.

"We are not spies," I said firmly in a loud, indignant voice. "We are here at the request of your leader to find out why people are getting sick. You will let us go through, right now, or you'll be in a lot of trouble. I promise you that. Lower that rifle and let us through!"

He blinked his eyes and glanced at his compatriots, who were equally as unsure. Handing back my credentials and passport, he meekly replied, "Yes sir. You may go. I am sorry."

Later that week we found ourselves at the top of a hill in the capital, Kampala. Millions of people had poured out into the parks and yards, rooftops and streets, to herald the arrival of the rebel leader, Yoweri Museveni, and his victorious army. As I shot video from that elevated position, we heard an enormous cheer erupt from the waiting crowd, and it appeared from our vantage point that a sole figure of a man was levitating above the mass of humanity. Even from that distance I could see that he was waving with both arms as he seemed to float along through his admirers. Then his motorcade turned toward the hill on which we stood, and it became obvious he was standing in the back of an open jeep.

The convoy of military vehicles and assorted pickup trucks drew to a stop near the top of the hill, and the future president climbed down. As he walked past us, Museveni's eyes met mine, and he looked momentarily surprised. A makeshift podium had been hastily assembled and a microphone attached to loudspeakers turned on. Museveni began speaking in the local dialects of Luganda and Swahili. Every thirty seconds or so the crowd erupted in approval.

At about the half-hour mark in his speech, Museveni turned in our direction and said something I couldn't understand, but a million or so pairs of eyes swiveled from looking at him to looking at us. There was a murmur from the crowd, and then applause. A man standing next to me leaned in close. "He say, 'This is a great day for our nation. And we welcome the presence of members of the international press to mark this important event.'" The "international press" consisted of a handful of freelancers. The rest of the world ignored third-world regime changes. When was the last time you saw a report about anything that happened on that continent that wasn't about a scary emerging disease or horrific famine? Such was Africa's lot.

History is rarely predictable. Most of the time it's a moment we stumble upon, not realizing its importance. That afternoon I was an accidental witness to the end of a terrible war and a new beginning for the people of Uganda. Unfortunately, after being heralded as part of a new generation of democratic African leaders, Yoweri Museveni devolved into an oppressive dictator whose primary focus became clinging to power rather than guiding his country back to economic and social progress. He was elected president six times, under a cloud of corruption including ballot box stuffing and human rights violations. But I'm betting you never saw that on your evening newscast.

There are still times I think about that boy at the checkpoint. And I truly hope he was able to lay down his rifle and go back to school. If he survived the war, and the AIDS epidemic, he'd be around forty years old now. I was lucky I guessed right with him that day. After most likely being conscripted at an early age into a violent, dehumanizing childhood, he's due some luck of his own.

A postscript to that trip. My fellow journalists and I finished our assignment and were seated in a Kenya Airways jet at Entebbe International Airport awaiting a short hop to Nairobi when a group of very loud, very unhappy athletes got on board. It was the Libyan national football (soccer) team, which had just been soundly beaten by Uganda's best. They filled in every available empty seat on the plane, including those among our little team of Americans.

This was just a few months after President Ronald Reagan ordered the bombing of Libya's capital, Tripoli, in retaliation for a Gaddafi-ordered terrorist attack on a Berlin nightclub that killed two American soldiers and injured seventy-nine others. As the Libyan athletes settled into their seats, a few began to notice the three white faces among their fellow passengers.

"American?" one asked me. I nodded. He introduced himself as the team's coach.

The largest member of their team leaned over to my fellow photographer, a longtime friend whose name I'll withhold to spare him some embarrassment. "And you, are you an American too?" the Libyan demanded.

My friend was the picture of innocence. "No spraken ze English," said the Iowa-born, nonbilingual Yank. "Ein German man."

I stifled a laugh. The coach chuckled. "You know," he said, "I think we should put our president and your president in a boxing ring together and let them go at it. Leave the rest of us in peace."

Indeed.

CHAPTER 19

A DOG NAMED SKYE

"We call him 'Wild Puppy,'" the lady said, as the tiny black-and-white border collie strutted forward from where his clutch of more timid brothers and sisters huddled. Weighing all of maybe one and a half pounds, the fluffy little smidgen came right up to me without an ounce of fear and sniffed my outstretched hand, tail wagging, eyes bright. There was never a doubt that this was our boy. He'd made his choice.

It was a working sheep farm, and these were the offspring of working sheep dogs, imported from Scotland, considered the smartest breed of dogs in the world. Naively, we thought a border collie would be a wonderful, fun pet. I mean, come on, the dogs in the movie *Babe* were nearly human!

To be clear, we soon learned border collies are not pets. They are Management.

On the drive home we couldn't decide on a name for him. Back in Charlotte, with a group of close friends who took turns cuddling the new baby, various suggestions were tossed about. But it was Fiona Ritchie, host of NPR's Celtic music program, *The Thistle & Shamrock*, who won the day. "Every time I'm on the Isle of Skye, I see a border collie lying on the front porch as if he just put away the sheep, balanced the ledger, and finished making dinner." So Skye it was.

All the other dogs I'd had in life were low maintenance. The miniature Schnauzer named Bobo and the Great Dane named Capri were easily house trained and understood the hierarchy of human/canine interactions. Skye had other ideas.

From the beginning he decided that it was he who would determine where his humans were going. If one of us got up from the couch and started toward the kitchen, Skye would dash ahead to lead. Bedtime? Skye led the way. The park? Don't you dare try to hold him back on a leash. He grasped the concept of catching a Frisbee on the fly when he was just a few months old, and we eventually competed all over the area, with him doing flips midair or launching off my shoulders. He could sit, lie down, speak, roll over, and flop down "dead" on command when you pretended to shoot him, staying perfectly still until I issued the release command. It was amazing how fast he could pick up new tricks. I would entertain our guests with his incredible math abilities, where I'd ask them to throw out any basic addition or subtraction problem, and he could solve it instantly, always barking the correct answer. Full disclosure—what our guests couldn't see was me, repeatedly making a fist by my side, which cued him to bark until the right number was reached.

It was also amazing how destructive he could be. He annihilated an entire couch when we left him for more than an hour. I came home to a room full of fluffy white stuffing. He dug through a Sheetrock wall during a thunderstorm, snapping off two of his toenails. He figured out how to open the pantry door and plunder anything and everything within. One memorable evening, he leapt on top of our coffee table in front of our dear friends David Murray and Linda Pattillo, sending cards and plastic pieces flying, fully disrupting an intense, hours-long Risk game, because we weren't paying him enough attention.

I quickly realized I was not equipped to control this intelligent bundle of energy. I found a highly recommended dog trainer who used a fairly new method of behavior modification to try to show our young pup the way. "Distract and praise" was his mantra. Interrupt the bad actions and praise the good. Show him you're the alpha dog.

I was, of course, skeptical.

First lesson: when I was walking to a particular room and he dashed ahead, I was to change course, no matter what, to demonstrate to him that he follows me, not the other way around. Skye really, really hated that one. He took to nipping me on the heels, like an errant ewe, when I spun and headed in the next direction. It took a good two weeks of daily work to get that to stick.

But after a lot of effort, Skye began to see the writing on the wall. To a point. He was still a nervous wreck during thunderstorms no matter how I dealt with it. He became a demolition expert if we locked him in the bathroom or garage. Veterinarian-prescribed sedatives simply left him in a stupor, lying in his own pee. A metal crate was suggested. He ripped out one of his canines trying to break out, leaving blood everywhere. All I could do was hold him tight during storms when I happened to be home and pray that the damage would be minimal when I wasn't.

We moved to the New York area when Sara James, my first wife, landed a terrific job with NBC News. Sara, by the way, is one of the best, sweetest, and smartest people I've ever had the honor of knowing. The fact that, as friends, we should never have married takes nothing away from how incredible this woman is. We divorced shortly after moving north. She found an apartment in the city; I took over the antique Queen Anne Victorian in New Jersey that was badly in need of repairs.

One night while I was out of town on a shoot, our beloved dog sitter, Elaine Fernandez, came over just as the thunder began and couldn't find him. Near as she could tell he dug his way out of the fenced-in yard in a panic. She hopped in her car and began driving around the neighborhood, shouting his name as the rain and wind began to diminish. Suddenly a passing police cruiser waved her to a stop.

"Hi! Are you looking for this guy?" the Glen Ridge cop asked, motioning to the back seat, where Skye sat, completely calm and content, looking at Elaine with a goofy smile.

"Yes, thank you so much! He hates thunderstorms."

"No kidding. We were patrolling the neighborhood before it hit, and all of a sudden this dog jumps through our open back window. Scared the crap out of us."

Without missing a beat, Elaine quipped, "Yeah. His owner taught him if he ever gets scared to go find a policeman."

Thus began the local legend of Skyedog.

From that moment on, the cops would often stop by to say hi to him, give him a treat, even toss a ball. We walked in the Memorial Day parade together and handed out candy on Halloween. The neighborhood kids started ringing the doorbell to ask if Skye could come out to play, and I'd watch them throw a Frisbee for him in the front yard. Over time, when the number of kids grew to six or eight, Skye took it on himself to organize the game. He hated chaos. He'd herd them into a neat line and hand the Frisbee to each one in order. If someone, by chance, grabbed the disc out of turn, Skye would gently take it from him or her and hand it to whomever was next in line.

One day, while I was about twenty feet off the ground on a ladder replacing the roof on the old house I was restoring on Woodland Avenue, I felt something brush my leg and glanced back to see my dog, big smile on his face, clinging to the rungs behind me. He'd watched me climb up and down a few dozen times and decided that looked like something fun to do.

What dog does that? He climbed a damn ladder! Carrying him down under one arm while trying not to fall and kill us both was, uh, interesting.

Skye had quickly become my best friend. I was traveling every month or so for CBS's *48 Hours* in those days, so

Elaine took care of my boy while I was away. But when I was home, it was the two of us, going everywhere, eating at local restaurants, running for five miles in the early morning calm. Tucked into each other on the couch with a book or TV show. There was nothing I did he didn't believe he could be a part of. And he was almost always right. There was an intelligence in those brown eyes, an understanding of *me*, that I've never known before or since.

Back then, my brother and I shared ownership of a cabin in Colorado that our father had built on the South Platte River, about an hour and a half west of Colorado Springs. It was in constant need of upkeep, and Erik and I took turns spending weeks at a time replacing stairs or rebuilding the fireplace or painting the exterior.

For me, it was a salve to the pressures of my professional life. The constant splash of the river, squawks of the blue jays, the ceaseless whisper of wind in the pines was calming. There, I slept the sleep of the dead. There, I had free time to read or think or write. Whenever I had a long enough break, I'd load Skye into my Ford Bronco, and we'd head west.

The Rocky Mountains are dog heaven. Skye reveled in chasing chipmunks or climbing the big hill behind the cabin. When I ventured into the river with waders and a fly rod, Skye would dash up and down the shore, desperate to figure out a way to join me. He'd finally muster up the courage to try swimming to where I was, only to look at me in dismay as the swift current would take him downstream. He quickly learned the command: "Go to the bank!" We would enjoy fresh trout for dinner every day.

I got a job offer from CNBC, and he moved with me to LA, fathered some pups of his own, and taught them how to swim in a pool. A few years later ABC News made me its national correspondent based in New York. Skye remained behind with his doggie family at the home of a close friend until my life (somewhat) settled down enough for me to bring him east. My girlfriend (and future wife) Katie Thomas and I rented a van and took him on a bucket list trip, stopping at Vegas, the Grand Canyon, and, yes, the cabin. He was no longer able to run up and down the mountain or swim in the river, but I could tell he remembered the place.

It's hard to watch your friends become old. The athlete who could once leap eight feet in the air to catch a Frisbee could now barely make it up the three flights of stairs to our Manhattan rental. Even so, he cherished his walks around the neighborhood and made friends with everyone there, especially the firemen at Engine 7/ Ladder 1, who always came out to greet him.

There came a time, inevitably, when Skye could no longer walk because of the crippling arthritis in his hips and ankles. He was fifteen years old, ancient for a working dog, and his body was failing. We tried everything to ease his pain, but it became an unavoidable realization that we'd have to say good-bye. I couldn't bear the thought that he was suffering.

When the appointed morning came, I picked him up and carried him down the stairs of our building, with Katie walking alongside us. I couldn't contain the tears. It was the single most difficult thing I've ever done. The veterinarian's office was a few blocks down the street, and I held him in my arms the whole way. When we arrived, we were taken into an examination room and given a few moments to say our goodbyes. Like most dogs, he hated going to the vets. But as he lay on the metal table that day, he looked at me with those huge, intuitive brown eyes, and I was surprised to see they were placid—not concerned, not scared, not anxious. He licked my hand as if to say, "It's okay. It's time." The shot was administered, and he fell asleep. I cry about that day every time I remember it, even as I write this.

But I saved the most amazing Skye story for last. One you may or may not choose to believe.

It happened back in Glen Ridge when he was in his prime. I was away on a trip. Elaine had taken to bringing Skye with her on all her dog sitting rounds because he was a calming influence on the other animals. He would settle fights, play with new pups, and show them the ropes.

One afternoon, Elaine and Skye were on their way to care for a little dog whose elderly owners were away for a few days when, a few blocks away, Skye began barking with alarm. It was a behavior none of us had ever witnessed from him, before or since, and Elaine couldn't calm him down. He was in a pure panic.

When she pulled into the couple's driveway, Skye didn't wait for her to come to a stop. He leapt out of the open window and ran to the front door, still barking. Elaine caught up to him and opened the door, and he dashed past her and ran room to room. She heard more barking upstairs and hurried up to where he stood in a bedroom. On the floor lay one of the little dog's owners, who came home from the trip early but had collapsed from a medical issue. Elaine immediately called an ambulance.

The old man survived.

I have no explanation for what happened that day.

CHAPTER 20

ELVIS HAS LEFT THE BUILDING

The house is a little disappointing when you first see it. Don't get me wrong; the colonial revival mansion is stately and sits regally behind the ornate gates, pink Alabama fieldstone wall, immaculate landscaping, and winding driveway, but at first glance, the most revered and most visited private home in America doesn't quite match up to its reputation. It seems to be, well, just a very nice, big house.

In 1992, my longtime friend and mentor Van Payne and I were hired to make a documentary about the fifteenth anniversary of Elvis Presley's death. His estate put us up in a trailer parked behind Graceland for a week of shooting, and we had almost total access to the house and grounds, with one exception: we weren't permitted to videotape anywhere on the second floor, where the king of rock 'n' roll had died of a heart attack while ignominiously sitting on the toilet.

Over the next few days we conducted interviews with his family and friends, filmed the nightly vigils held by tens of thousands of fans outside the gates, and took carefully lit videos of the Jungle Room, his walls of gold records, and even the snowmobiles he had converted into go-carts on which he and his cohorts used to careen around the fourteen-acre estate. I pored over biographies and old home movies and photographs, some of which would be surprising to all but the most knowledgeable of fans—such as the fact that he was born a natural blond and dyed his hair, eyebrows, and even lashes dark black for the rest of his life.

I had been aware of Elvis's music, of course, even though I couldn't admit to being much of a fan. But that week we immersed ourselves in his entire catalogue so that we could select the perfect soundtrack for the program, and I quickly grew to appreciate his enormous talent and his incredible voice. "Kentucky Rain," "A Little Less Conversation," "In the Ghetto," "Suspicious Minds," and especially his phenomenal performance of "If I Can Dream" during his 1968 "comeback special" are nothing less than extraordinary.

Van and I feasted on Memphis barbecue and fresh-caught catfish. I even tried Elvis's favorite sandwich—banana, bacon, and peanut butter on white bread—but could never muster up as much affection for it as he did.

After Presley's death, his family almost lost Graceland to the federal government. They owed $500,000 in taxes, and his entire estate had been gradually reduced to a value of only twice that amount. Desperate to save it, his executor and former wife, Priscilla Presley, hired a CEO and opened the mansion up to the public. Within a month the estate was in the black, and it eventually earned Priscilla's and Elvis's daughter, Lisa Marie, a trust of over $100 million. It was revealed upon Lisa Marie's untimely death that the value had ballooned to almost half a billion, which she left to her own children.

On our last night there, I finally ginned up the courage to slip up the stairs to the second floor and take a quick look around. The rooms were a somber contrast to the downstairs, which had been carefully maintained just as it was when Elvis lived there. Instead, the bedrooms were full of cardboard boxes and cloth-covered furniture. The master bedroom was also being used for storage, but I could still see, mounted in the ceiling above the large bed, three TVs he used to watch all his favorite sports while lying flat on his back.

I chose not to go looking for the infamous bathroom. It seemed a disrespectful intrusion. In a world of people who are famous simply for being famous, Elvis Presley was the real thing. A beautiful, talented man who rose above the humblest of beginnings to become musical royalty.

On the anniversary of his death, the ornate gates were opened to tens of thousands of his fans. They filed up the driveway and quietly made their way in a procession around his grave before circling back down to the street. The next morning, workers didn't find a single piece of trash on the grounds.

CHAPTER 21

ARE WE ALONE?

I didn't want to call him, but I was out of options. There were too many roadblocks, too many layers of obfuscation. The Pentagon was not being at all helpful.

My dad answered on the second ring. "Hello." The familiar voice immediately brought back the old feelings of anxiety and defensiveness. I hadn't seen him in person for years, but my stomach still clinched when he spoke.

"Hi dad, it's me."

"Dutch!" That was my family nickname. "How ya doin' son? It's been a while."

"Good, good…" I chatted with him awhile, catching him up on things, asking about his life. Then, before the conversation could shift, as it inevitably would, to politics or his lectures about what was wrong with the world at large and the mainstream media in particular, I got to the purpose of the call.

"Dad, I'm doing an investigation of UFOs for CBS News's *48 Hours*. A serious one. They want me to see if I can find any authentic evidence of extraterrestrial visits."

I'd already gathered hours of witness interviews, video recordings of unusual aircraft, and even a handful of small, shiny, metallic beads from an alleged "crash site" in Russia, the molecular makeup of which a lab had, as of that year, been unable to identify.

I heard him chuckle. "That's what they're paying you for, huh? Might as well be a reporter for the *National Enquirer*."

I ignored the insult. "No major news network has taken an objective look at the issue, so we're trying to cut through all the baloney and see what has really happened."

"OK. Well, what can I do for you? I've never seen one."

"The base commander at Wright-Patt while you were there. Do you still have his contact information?"

"I think so. Hold on while I go look."

He placed the phone handset on the table with a *thunk*. Three minutes later, the former Air Force colonel returned. "Got it." I could hear him ruffling through the pages of his address book before reading off the man's name, address, and phone numbers. "That last one is his home number. But I'm sure he's retired by now. He's a few years older than me."

"That's OK. At least it's a start. Thanks so much."

We said our goodbyes, promised to stay in touch, and clicked off. I dialed the first number and was connected to Wright-Patterson Air Force Base. The person politely informed me that the general was, in fact, retired. My request for forwarding information was politely denied.

Wright-Patterson, you may recall, is the place that allegedly stored and studied the wreckage of a UFO that, legend has it, went down in 1947 near Area 51 in Roswell, New Mexico. Rumors over the years claimed that one or more bodies of aliens were being kept in a secret facility on the base.

I dialed the second number. It took a few moments, but eventually a man answered in a scratchy voice. "Yes?"

"Hello, general. I'm sorry to bother you. My father used to work for you at Wright-Pat—Don Dahler." (I'm named after my dad.)

"Ah, yes! Don! How is he?" I sensed a tinge of dread in that last question, as if he anticipated news of another death among his aging contemporaries.

"He's fine. Good. Doing well. Living in San Antonio. Playing a lot of golf."

"Ah, he always did love that game. I took a lot of money off him when we played, though."

"Yeah, he was never very good."

"Do you ever get out with him?"

Never, I thought. Never once was I invited. But I replied, "Not nearly enough."

"Well, how can I help you?"

I gave him my rehearsed speech about our attempt to responsibly answer the many questions about UFOs that have existed for decades. As I spoke, I heard him let out a breath, but I couldn't discern if it was a sigh or snort of derision.

When I finished, he paused for a long moment, then said, "If you weren't Don's son, I would've hung up the moment you mentioned UFOs. But all I'll tell you is this: when I first took command of the base, I had to sign a nondisclosure agreement. If I was ever to break that agreement, I could lose my pension and my rank and even possibly go to prison. So I can't tell you anything, and you can't use my name in your report." He took a moment to let that sink in. "But the question you should be asking is: why would they make me sign that if there was nothing there?"

He wished me good luck, asked that I give Dad his best, told me to not call back, and hung up.

CHAPTER 22

SPY VERSUS SPY

The greying, middle-aged man emerged from his multimillion-dollar Bel Air mansion and walked slowly to his mailbox. I triggered my video camera and began filming. Seeing me parked across the street, Ronald J. Hoffman offered a limp wave before retrieving his mail and heading back inside. It was obvious he was not at all surprised to see me. Considering the rocket scientist was under investigation for selling top secret software to other governments through his defense contracting firm, Plume Technology, he likely assumed I was a federal officer keeping an eye on him. I have no earthly idea how he came to that conclusion.

OK, so I might have resembled a fed. I was dressed in a dark suit, dark tie, dark sunglasses. I had a pair of large binoculars noticeably stationed on the dash of my nondescript white Crown Victoria rental. It took sixteen calls to rental companies in the LA area before I found the one I wanted, the one that looked like every other government-issued vehicle on the road in the early '90s.

Whenever the private security patrols rolled by, they wouldn't even bother to ask what I was doing there. They'd give me a friendly nod of the head and keep on moving. Had they stopped and asked for identification, I would have told them I was a producer working for CBS News's *48 Hours* investigating a story about a scientist accused of attempting to sell "Star Wars" (a missile defense program, called the Strategic Defense Initiative, that was started under Ronald Regan) technology to a handful of countries, including Japan. As Bel Air is a gated community, I would have fully expected them to then escort me to the big gates at the entrance and tell me to never come back. Instead, they assumed I was a federal officer. Which was the entire purpose of my getup.

To be clear, I would never tell someone I was a law enforcement officer under any circumstances. (Unlike one bozo, a New York–based reporter, who in the days after 9/11 donned a Bureau of Alcohol, Tobacco, Firearms, and Explosives cap and tried to pass himself off as a federal agent to gain access to ground zero. He allegedly told a National Guardsman he'd lost his ATF identification. The reporter was arrested, but the charges were dismissed.) There are clear lines that should never be crossed. *Looking* like an agent, though, and *falsely identifying* oneself as an agent are two very different things.

Hoffman had been a tough man to get video of, which is why I was forced to figure out how to stake out his house in such an exclusive community. Sitting in my rental car, I photographed him coming and going, working in his yard, and driving past me on his way to the marina, from which he sailed his yacht. Back in those days, *48 Hours* had a healthy budget, so I was able to hire a helicopter and get lovely aerials of him competing in a regatta.

At this point you may be asking yourself: How does a scientist afford a mansion, a big sailboat, and expensive cars? Maybe the $150,000 check he accepted from an undercover officer in return for a disk containing SDI software gives you some clue. At one point during a meeting with agents posing as South Africans, he got suspicious. A law enforcement source told me he can be heard on tape saying, "If you're a federal agent, you have to tell me. That's the law."

Note to aspiring criminals—no, it's not.

Eventually, I convinced him over the phone to be interviewed, to tell his side of the story and counter the government's assertions. He was, understandably, nervous on the day of the interview, and during every break as the cameramen changed tapes and batteries, he looked at me earnestly and said, "I don't think this is going well."

It wasn't. Not for him, anyway. With every claim of "public domain software" or "entrapment," I could produce refuting documentation. But I just urged him, "Show us that passion you had over the phone. This is your chance to get your side on the record." I actually felt sorry for him. But I didn't want him to pull the plug on the interview and kick us out of his house before we got everything we needed.

Ron Hoffman was eventually convicted on numerous charges and sentenced to two and a half years in prison and a hefty fine.

CHAPTER 23

FAKE NEWS

"I'm a great judge of talent!" the elderly man yelled after me as two security guards escorted me down the hall and out of the building, "And mark my words! You'll end up selling shoes for a living!"

I'd just slapped a script on Chet Collier's desk and told the news network's number two that either he either let me out of my contract, or a copy of that script, and the notations made by the company's vice president, would be on its way to the *New York Times*. I had intended to confront the cable channel's founder and president, but Roger Ailes was away on a business trip.

I was one of Fox News Channel's first hires. As the investigative correspondent, I reported on issues such as human smuggling across the Mexican border. Because of the sensitive nature of some of my assignments, I answered directly to the VP of newsgathering, John Moody, a former bureau chief for *Time* magazine. Viewership numbers those first few months were miniscule—nothing like the millions of deluded fans who tune in now for their daily helping of misinformation, manipulation, and fearmongering, but we went about our business as if we were already a legitimate competitor to the other cable news operations. Full disclosure: when I took the job, I had no idea what the hidden agenda was. But after a few questionable edits to my well-researched and vetted reports, it became apparent that facts were less important than a certain point of view. When, after seeing the handwriting on the wall a few months in, I first asked to be released from my three-year contract, I was told, "Absolutely not," with no explanation or discussion. I asked again, and again, with no luck.

Then I got the assignment to work up a multipart report on why Americans were so discouraged about the state of the nation, and does reality match the perception. I was told to specifically take a hard look at affirmative action—where had it failed, where had it succeeded. I spent the better part of a month poring over Census figures, Department of Labor reports, crime statistics, and college enrollment data and interviewing half a dozen experts. I honestly had no idea where my research would lead, but ultimately it showed that, in the mean, affirmative action was achieving or exceeding almost all of its stated goals, with the two glaring failures being Black-on-Black crime rates and Black male college graduations. Black female graduations were at an all-time high.

Per protocol, I submitted the scripts for my five-part report to Moody and waited. Two days later he sent them back, with numerous cross outs and added sentences. I was sincerely dismayed and sent them right back with a note saying, in effect, "These changes are inaccurate and not what my reporting found."

That's when he screwed up. The scripts came back to me that very day. In bright red marker he'd written, at the bottom, "Our constituents will not appreciate what you're reporting."

Constituents?

Silly me. I thought our job was to simply try to find out the truth, as much as we could. I never thought of our viewers as constituents. And I certainly didn't have a personal dog in the "affirmative action: good or bad?" fight.

After making copies of the scripts, including his comment, sending one to my agent, and putting the others in a safe place (I still have a copy), I took the elevator up to the executive floor, where I was informed that Ailes, later exposed as an alleged serial sexual abuser, was away, but his faithful lieutenant was in and available to talk.

The conversation devolved rapidly. "This isn't about journalism," Collier sneered. "That's what you don't understand. This is about business. We're in the news *business*. That means finding as many customers for the advertisers as you can. We're selling what these ignored people want to hear. And what you wrote here will not make our customers happy."

"I'm not selling anything," I replied. "I try to find out what's really happening. I have no political agenda. Hell, I don't even like politics."

"Then you chose the wrong career. Every news outlet has an agenda. They're pushing their own angle on things. It's a fact. They're all biased. We're just filling a void in the marketplace."

I'd already worked for one national news network and would work for two more in the years ahead. Never before nor again did an executive or producer ever pressure me to change my reporting to fit an agenda, political or otherwise. The news media without question struggles with unintentional bias, driven by personal history and education, but I would state under oath in a court of law that I have never been subject to deliberate manipulation of a story for political reasons—except at that particular cable news network.

Collier yelled out the door for his personal assistant to call security. The two nice men politely marched me out the large, glass doors and onto Sixth Avenue, where I stood for a moment, assessing my new reality: unemployed, not much money in the bank, and no job prospects in sight. I'd been there before and somehow came out ahead. I was fairly sure I could do so again. Fairly sure. Within two weeks I was headed west to work for CNBC out of its Burbank bureau as a West Coast correspondent.

A few short years later, when it was announced I was the new national correspondent for ABC News, I sent a gift box with an enclosed note card to Chet Collier. Inside was a pair of shoes.

"Thanks for the professional advice," the note read.

CHAPTER 24

THE MAN, THE MYTH, THE MARY JANE

The door opened, momentarily spilling a shaft of light into the darkened theater, and then quietly closed. A dark figure moved past and settled into the plush leather chair directly behind me. I turned my attention once again to the prereleased movie a small group of us were screening in Robert Evans's luxurious home theater.

Evans, as he liked to be called, was a legendary Hollywood producer who had shepherded a string of hits while head of Paramount Pictures: *Rosemary's Baby*, *Love Story*, *The Godfather*, and *Chinatown*, to name just a few. For three decades, his handsome, ever-tanned visage was *the* face of the business of American cinema. His own life story, the majestic heights and terrible lows, is beautifully told in his autobiography, *The Kid Stays in the Picture*, and its concomitant documentary by Brett Morgen. Through mutual friends I'd come to know Evans, whose lovely Beverly Hills mansion was nestled within the trees and ivy-covered gates a few blocks down the street from my much humbler rental house. Once or twice a week he would sit next to his private tennis court, cocktail and cigarette at the ready, while I hit with his personal coach. Evans loved tennis but could no longer play due to health issues. His comments and jokes kept the sessions laugh filled, and I cherished those moments.

I was one of CNBC's West Coast correspondents at the time, working out of its Burbank studios. It was a low-paying but rewarding job, and because the shows I was reporting for were all off the air by around 3:00 p.m. LA time, my afternoons were largely free for tennis, or surfing or kayaking in the waves off Santa Monica. On weekends I would play in pickup basketball games at the local high school with the likes of a young up-and-coming actor by the name of George Clooney, who had a nifty fadeaway jumper. I went to parties with Gene Simmons and Paul Stanley of *KISS*, whose quiet, gentlemanly personalities were the opposite of their bombastic stage performances. During dinner one evening at Ellen DeGeneres's Hancock Park home with her girlfriend at the time, Anne Heche, and my girlfriend at the time, Giselle Fernandez, Ellen, who may or may not be a distant cousin of mine, took my hand in hers and asked if I'd be willing to donate my sperm so that she and Anne could have a baby. Ultimately I couldn't accept the privacy restrictions they required, such as the child never knowing I was his/her father, but I was deeply flattered. In retrospect it also shows just how strange my years in La-La Land were.

Hollywood is an insular fraternity, where even stars and executives—whose introductions now include the adjective *former*—enjoy some measure of privilege. Evans hadn't been a studio chief in years, but he was still on the distribution list for screeners of movies that had yet to be released, and he enjoyed gathering small groups of friends to hold court in his theater and pass judgment on the newest films. I can't remember what the title was that evening, but it was bad. Really bad. In the darkened rooms I could catch the occasional moan or chuckle over a particularly awkward bit of acting.

A few moments after the person sat down behind me, I smelled the distinctive odor of marijuana, and a familiar voice declared, "Well, this is a complete load of crap." He then began ad-libbing his own dialogue for every character on screen, even the women. It was fall-down hilarious. A thousand times better than the actual film. My stomach hurt from laughing. Evans called for his projectionist to turn down the volume and let the great actor riff his way through the remainder of the movie. Every once in a while, the doobie appeared over my shoulder, an offering from the legend. I can neither confirm nor deny that I partook.

That actor was Jack Nicholson.

CHAPTER 25

MOUNTAIN OF DEATH

Through the fluttering canvas, I saw Don standing in the rain by the car. He had already donned his poncho and a special waterproofed Australian-style hat. I could barely see his face, momentarily highlighted by the truck's oversized red taillights. His ghastly expression lingered, permanently etched in my mind, as we rolled away. I waved, but he couldn't see me. Still I waved long after he dropped completely out of sight. I had a horrible sensation that I would never see him again. I felt the loss as if it had already happened.

That paragraph is from the book *Shadowcatchers* by Steve Wall, which is about our difficult, sometimes dangerous journey together in search of the teachings of indigenous healers. Steve is an extraordinary man—spiritual, intellectual, passionate, and a gifted *National Geographic* photographer. He also coauthored the bestseller *Wisdomkeepers* with former *Geographic* senior editor Harvey Arden—a collection of interviews with Native American tribal elders throughout the US—among many other interesting works.

Steve happens to be deathly terrified of airplanes. That was why, in 1993, we had decided on traveling overland to Central America via the infamous Pan-American Highway. Our plan was to load up my Ford Bronco four-wheel drive with supplies and journey down through Mexico into Guatemala, Belize, Honduras, El Salvador, Nicaragua, Costa Rica, and Panama, stopping at various villages where the elders, who carried with them the knowledge of their people's beliefs, traditions, and medicine, could be found. Unfortunately, the Bronco broke down just before our departure date. So Steve was forced to face his fears, and we ended up flying on separate airplanes to Costa Rica, where we rented a bright-red Suzuki Sidekick to tackle the grueling mountain passes, muddy hillsides, and pot-holed local goat paths euphemistically called "roads." Which brings us to that moment in that particular passage when I was standing in the torrential rain next to our disabled vehicle on what the locals had dubbed Cerro de la Muerte, "Mountain of Death," the highest point on the Pan-American Highway, as Steve disappeared into the mist aboard a pickup truck we'd waved down in order to find a tire repair shop. I watched the taillights fade into the dark and wondered how many things could go wrong on a single project. We'd narrowly missed plunging down the side of the mountain yet again when one of the trillion potholes I tried to weave my way around shredded two of our vehicle's tires. That was definitely not the high point of the trip.

National Geographic television agreed to partially sponsor me for a scout trip to see if a full documentary could be developed from what Steve and I could find, and I talked Costa Rica's national airline, LACSA, into discounted flights and accommodations in return for writing some travel articles for US publication. All that helped with expenses, but even so there was no guarantee of making any money from the many months of effort. Steve was on deadline for his book; I was on deadline to get traction in my documentary career. I was also finding any excuse to be away from home, away from an unhappy marriage with a cloudy future.

Sara and I never fought. I can't remember a single argument. She was beautiful and kind and funny and smart. And despite all those marvelous attributes, I wasn't in love with her. The friendship that was born in Richmond should have stayed just that—a friendship. But I—perhaps because of a realization that, with my many travels and risks taken abroad and a crippled relationship with my parents, there was really no one who would know or care whether I survived the adventures I so craved; no one to mourn me; no one to remember me—convinced myself that the romantic feelings would grow in time to become what they should have been from the beginning. And, yes, I was fooling myself. Ultimately my selfishness cost her considerable pain, and me a good friend. The only consolation I have for what I did to her is knowing she eventually found love and built a wonderful life for herself in Australia.

That near-death experience on the Mountain of Death happened a few days after Steve and I were tossed from our beds in the middle of the night in San José by an earthquake, one of the 350 that hit Costa Rica every month. There are not many more perfect metaphors for the trip, except, perhaps, for the moment I lifted a weary sloth from the middle of the road and carried him out of danger to a tree while he kept trying, in slow motion, to slash me with his claws. Seemingly every step of the way was met with obstacles, missed appointments, misunderstandings, and tension. For various reasons we ended up traveling separately for much of the journey, although in those times I always missed Steve's insights and humor. There are some people tuned into a higher frequency of awareness. Steve Wall is one of them.

I'd grown up in Texas speaking passable Spanish, but I was in no way fluent enough for Steve's purposes, so he used locals both as guides and translators. Even so, when I was off on my own, I was surprised by how quickly my vocabulary and ear for the language rebounded. In English, the consonants are most important; in Spanish, it's the vowels. After three weeks of total immersion, I was happy to realize I had begun dreaming in Spanish.

I spent a total of about two months wandering around Central America—taking part in a Mayan ceremony that lasted all night; hiking three days into the Monteverde cloud forest with an American expat who'd been imprisoned for refusing to fight in the Korean War; interviewing a Miskito activist, Brooklyn Rivera, who is now a member of the Nicaraguan government; and crossing the Mountain of Death a total of six knee-knocking, white-knuckled times. My journal is full of the stories and legends and philosophies generously passed on by the elders and activists and healers and transplants I met, but as a respectful admission that Steve chronicled their stories in his book much better than I ever could, I won't repeat them here—with the exception of one encounter that reminds me *wisdom* is not always a product of higher education.

Braulio Morales greeted me at the door of the small grey house he'd built himself and invited me to come meet his chickens. A dozen of them clucked around our feet as we sat on some large truck tires to talk. Occasionally, the goose he keeps to protect the flock wandered over to peck at the brass fasteners on my camera bag. "Watch out for him," the seventy-seven-year-old member of Costa Rica's Boruca tribe warned me. "He is a mean one." Just as he spoke, a three-inch-long grasshopper with bright yellow eyes and wings that resembled leaves of grass climbed onto my leg. In a flash, the goose pounced, swallowing the grasshopper whole.

Braulio was a slight man with creases around his eyes that spread like ripples on a pond when he found something amusing. "I'm one of only two people in this village who still know how to speak Boruca," he said. "The schools for many years only taught Spanish. But now there is an effort to teach our children the native language to preserve it. For the government, though, it's not a priority." He motioned toward a tin-roofed building up the dirt road with an attached thirty-foot tall antenna. "That is Radio Boruca. It used to broadcast in our language. Now it just plays American music."

Braulio is also the last one on the mountain who knows how to build houses the old way, weaving straw into mats for the roof. For a time he tried to recruit other young men in the area to learn, but no one was interested, preferring wooden planks and galvanized steel. "My roof," he said, pointing at it, "will last sixty years. His"—motioning to that of his neighbor's—"will need to be replaced in six."

As we talked, his wife of fifty years tended their garden; a slender, petite woman whose grey hair darkened toward the ends of the two long pigtails that gave her a wistfully girlish appearance. Her glasses magnified a pair of large, expressive, kindly eyes. Braulio first met Doña Salina when he was six and she was still an infant in her basket. Salina told me she never knew her father. At the time of her birth, her mother was married to another man, who announced he would not keep the baby and told her to "throw her down the mountain." Instead, her mother hid her inside a loom, feeding her whenever she could sneak away. When the girl was a toddler, he grudgingly accepted that they couldn't murder the child. But, Salina said, her stepfather never said a word to her. Once she was weaned, her abuela took her in.

Braulio and Salina grew up as neighbors, but her grandmother would rarely let the girl out into public, much less talk to boys. At some point when he was about twenty-one, he realized she was the prettiest girl in the village and decided he would make her like him. Finally, after much negotiation, her abuela agreed to let him visit their house. As he and Salina sat across the room from each other, the grandmother, two aunts, and three other village women stood nearby, watching every move. Despite the restrictions, Braulio won her over, and they were married. Seven children, twenty-eight grandchildren, and fourteen great-grandchildren later, Braulio's only regret is that he loved to go out and dance, and Salina, traumatized by her oppressive upbringing, would only dance with him in the privacy of their tiny home. "Still," he said, with a twinkle in his eye, "she's a better dancer than me."

As the afternoon advanced, I caught sight of fleeting moments of affection between the two—a glance, a smile, a touch of an arm, a chuckle shared about some private joke or memory. During a walk down to the river to let some of the great-grandkids have a swim at the three waterfalls, we watched Salina skipping ahead, a tiny hand in each of hers. The seventy-three-year-old moved effortlessly down the steep path as if she were seventeen, pointing out the names of trees and plants to the young ones as they passed. I asked Braulio how they'd been able to stay happy together for so long.

Before he could answer, a black-and-white junco bird burst from the underbrush with a snake in its mouth, flapping up into the air. It had nearly reached the treetops when the snake wiggled free and began falling directly toward us. Six feet above our heads, the bird swooped in and grabbed it again. We could feel the wind from his wings as he hurried away with dinner.

"*Terciopelo,*" Braulio said, giving the local name for the brightly colored fer-de-lance snake, the most dangerous in Costa Rica, which almost landed on top of us. "Very poisonous. Many of our people have died from his bite. The junco must be your spirit animal. He protected you."

When we reached the falls, I asked again about his long life journey with Salina, and how they make it work, as the children laughed and splashed in the falls and his wife of five decades looked on, arms crossed, an enormous smile on her still-pretty face.

"People are different," he replied after giving it some thought. "I can't advise you as to what works in a marriage. Sometimes the problems are the man's fault—he beats the woman; sometimes problems are the woman's fault—she sees other man. But I think the main problem is when you believe your husband or wife is there only to serve you, make your life better. To give you happiness. In truth, marriage is a search for yourself."

CHAPTER 26

THE EVIL MEN DO

The ten-year-old boy had disheveled blond hair, the world's saddest eyes, and one arm in a cast. We were sitting in his hospital room in Pristina, Kosovo, as he told us about the day the Serbian militia came to his small village.

The men went house to house, he said through an interpreter, and shot all the adults who hadn't already fled the area. His own father had been killed months earlier near the Albanian border, one of the 13,500 people who perished during the two-year-long war. The non-Serbian population had risen up against Yugoslavian rule, which was marked by continuous and brutal oppression.

When the paramilitary unit got to the boy's house, they shot his mother without a word of warning and then shot him as he tried to escape through a window. He played dead, lying in the bushes, until the men set fire to the house.

The boy began to cry as he told us about trying to help his little sister—I believe he said she was only four—climb through the window to escape the flames, but the bullet had shattered his arm, and he couldn't reach her. He screamed for her to jump, but she wasn't strong enough to climb up and out. Finally, he said, the heat and smoke forced him to run away. The camera crew and I, all veterans of the cruelty and horrors of war, and this one in particular, could not stop the tears from flowing as we listened to the boy's story.

That was just one of thousands of war crimes committed by paramilitary forces in Kosovo, on both sides of the conflict. While covering the war, we heard far too many stories about this and saw far too many broken families. The Yugoslavian president, Slobodan Milošević, was eventually charged with genocide and crimes against humanity and extradited by the International Tribunal for the former Yugoslavia at The Hague, under intense pressure by the United States. The ICTY indictment said he was directly responsible for the forced deportation of 800,000 ethnic Albanians from Kosovo and the murders of thousands more. After a two-year-long trial, the former dictator and many of his compatriots, including Radovan Karadžić, were found guilty of numerous crimes by the international court.

Unfortunately, Milošević died in jail of natural causes before sentencing. He went to his grave unpunished for the sorrow and suffering he inflicted on millions of innocent people, including the little boy in that hospital bed. Many Serbs still consider him a national hero.

In the rubble of the World Trade Center.

Don anchoring the news for CBS Sunday
Morning. Photo courtesy of CBS News.

With Diane Sawyer of Good Morning America for the
Street Luge Race. Photo Courtesy of ABC News.

Filming a documentary with Charles Kuralt.
Photo courtesy of Van Payne.

Robin Roberts during the X-Treme Urban Challenge
on GMA. Photo courtesy of ABC News.

The Taekwondo National Championships.
Photo courtesy of Wan Pae Pak.

The boy who wanted adventures.

Skye.

The Tar Heel Traveler hiking through the woods of North Carolina.

Hang gliding over the Blue Ridge Mountains.

Hanging out with neighborhood kids and a chicken.
Photo courtesy of Joanna B. Pinneo.

Kokpar, a cross between polo and rugby.

Ascending after a free dive of 150 feet on live TV.

The Cairo camel market.

Dinner in Burkina Faso.

Kayaking in Malibu

Skulls lining the road in Luwero, Uganda.

Filming at the oasis.

The ellies.

Taking off with Des in the Drifter. Photo Courtesy of Jen Bartlett.

The Bartlett's camp at Ausis.

The compound and guards at Khoja Bahauddin.

Young Afghan soldier with the owl he shot.

Fording a river on the way to the front lines,
guided by a boy on horseback.

Back in camp after a day of house-to-house battles.

My desert office in Iraq.

Outside of Najaf.

Part of the 101st Airborne 2/502 Strike Force.

CHAPTER 27

SHAQ AND THE BLACK MAMBA

We sat down under the lights in one of the small conference rooms at the Staples Center after practice. Weeks of appeals from *Good Morning America*'s booking staff finally convinced the Lakers to agree to let me interview their newest star, a high school standout who'd led his Lower Merion, Pennsylvania, team to its first state championship in fifty-three years by averaging 30.8 points and 6.5 assists a game. Despite being heavily recruited by Duke, Michigan, North Carolina, and Villanova, the seventeen-year-old decided to enter the NBA draft. The rest is history.

The Charlotte Hornets got him first but immediately traded him to the Lakers, which happened to be his favorite childhood team. Since he was underage at the time, his parents had to cosign his contract, a three-year deal paying him a total of $3.5 million. By the end of his rookie season, Kobe Bryant demolished all doubts. He established himself as one of the preeminent shooting guards in the league and went on to become one of the greatest players and scorers in NBA history.

But when he walked into the room and ducked under the lights to shake my hand, he was the young, painfully shy, modest high schooler who was still amazed he had convinced the singer Brandy to accompany him to prom.

He was, even then, a strikingly attractive man. And that smile…effervescent and sincere. The entire crew and I were smitten by his humanity, humility, and quiet humor. Yet Kobe also projected enormous self-confidence. He knew what he could do. He knew what he was going to do. Of that, he had no doubt.

As we talked at length about his childhood growing up in Italy as his father, a former NBA player himself, grinded out the last few years of his career playing in Europe, he demonstrated his fluency in Italian and talked of his love for the game of soccer. He was proud of scoring a 1080 in the SATs and admitted he would have enjoyed playing for a college team, but that he felt he was ready to take on the pros.

It was around that point in the interview when a loud voice shattered the quiet and a hulking figure burst into the room: Shaquille O'Neal. He ducked past the cameras and light stands, grabbed Bryant, and lifted him out of his chair.

"This little guy here, my little brother, is the future of the Lakers!" he declared. "You guys just watch. We're going to win the championship, not just once, but lots of times. You just watch!"

He and Kobe wrestled around for a moment before he let Kobe go. There was real affection between the two, making their eventual falling-out even more painful to watch for those of us who were in the room at the time.

Shaq was right. Kobe eventually won five championship rings and two Olympic gold medals. Despite the disturbing accusations of rape in 2004, the charges of which were dismissed but settled out of court in the civil case, I and most of the rest of the world were devastated when he was killed in a helicopter crash in 2020. The Black Mamba was more than a great basketball player; he was a great man, a great father, a great soul. He had so much left to accomplish.

CHAPTER 28

IRONY IS DEAD

Heading up to the 2000 presidential election, *Good Morning America*'s executive producer, Shelley Ross, decided to do a series of profiles of the potential first ladies. ABC's vaunted political unit dispatched correspondents to interview Mesdames Gore, Bradley, McCain, Forbes, and Bush. I was assigned the girlfriend of a millionaire businessman who had not yet declared but was flirting with the prospect. She happened to be in New York City that week for a charity event—a photo shoot promoting pet adoptions—so a producer, camera crew, and I made our way to the midtown studio where the event was being held.

Melania Knauss was a twenty-six-year-old model from Slovenia who'd been dating then-fifty-three-year-old Donald Trump for about a year. As we chatted, she lounged on a red armchair, with a puppy cuddled in her arms. She seemed sweet and somewhat overwhelmed with the attention. When the actual interview began, her answers were a little more guarded, and when I pointed that out, she allowed that over the past twelve months, since Trump zeroed in on her at a New York Fashion Week gala, she had learned the media "can be very tricky sometimes. You need to be very careful."

Let's be clear. Not for one moment did I think Trump was serious about running for president. I don't think anybody did. In 2015, after he rode down the escalator in front of dozens of hired "supporters" to announce his candidacy, one of his key employees told me that Trump never expected to win, but the campaign would be enormously beneficial to his brand. Trump was better known in New York circles as a publicity hound who, somewhat pathetically, insisted on plastering his name on any and every building he could and making calls to reporters posing as his own imaginary publicist named John Barron, bragging about his sexual conquests. But Shelley Ross had the instincts of a tabloid newspaper editor—she could spot a juicy story from twenty paces, and a profile of the twice-divorced real estate mogul's newest arm candy was too much fun to pass up.

"Donald Trump's name is synonymous with a lot of things," I asked, "not the least of which is the phrase 'prenuptial agreement.' Given his history with acrimonious divorces, would you even consider signing one with him?"

She replied, in her now-familiar Slavic accent, "You know, everybody has different opinions, so let's see what happens."

When we got around to the topic of the upcoming election, she insisted her beau would be a "great president," and she was convinced he would eventually run, if not that year, then in the future. "He's very smart," she said. "He knows how to do a business. He would be a great leader."

"Can you picture yourself a first lady?" I asked.

"Yes. I would be very traditional. Like Jackie Kennedy. I would support him. I would do a lot of social obligations."

"Have you been hurt by the comments that you're with him because he's rich?"

"No, the people, they don't know me. People who talk like this, they don't know me."

I paused. "Well, you don't see many twenty-six-year-old supermodels on the arm of a fifty-two-year-old car mechanic."

She then showed her natural instinct for deflection. Without missing a beat, she explained you can't sleep with beautiful things, either a beautiful apartment or a car. She never did answer the actual question. "People who say those things don't know me."

She eventually married Trump in 2005. Ten years after I interviewed Melania, I sat down in the Donald's palatial office to talk to him about a new lawsuit that accused his Trump University of bilking its students out of thousands of dollars under false promises of an education in real estate from the very best in the business, a class action suit he eventually settled for $25 million.

My take on the future twice-impeached president that day was: I get it. I understand how he has managed to float above numerous financial catastrophes, bankruptcies, federal civil rights investigations, and personal scandals. The guy can really turn on the charm when he wants to. He was funny and complimentary, telling me he enjoyed watching me and that I should have my own show.

Every hard question I hit him with, every angry quote from a disgruntled student I read, every document I produced that contradicted his glib answer was met with a shrug and a flat denial. I realized during the interview that I could have shown him hidden camera video (had it existed) of him designing the grift with his top lieutenants, and he would still have looked me in the eye and said it was not true. He was never going to give me the truth and never going to admit fault.

I was reminded of that moment, years later, when President Trump batted away scandal after scandal, accusation after accusation, fact after fact. The man is incapable of taking responsibility for his crimes. He is a master of the bald-faced lie.

As for his beautiful wife, by the time she moved to the White House, the young, doe-eyed immigrant had a harder cast to her face. Her speech was more clipped. Her eyes constantly narrowed into slits of distrust. Their marriage had been blighted by constant reports of infidelity, his political campaign almost derailed by an admission caught on camera that he could "...do anything. Grab 'em by the p#@sy. When you're a star, they let you do it," and I wondered if she still thought of him as "kind."

I had asked her that day at the photo shoot if it bothered her that Trump referred to himself as a playboy.

"No," she smiled. "It's a man thing. And sometimes I find it very cute."

CHAPTER 29

OH, THE SHARK, BABE, HAS SUCH TEETH, DEAR

The Bahamian waters were warm and soft, even at 10:00 a.m. I pulled up the top of my wet suit and began shrugging on various pieces of dive gear before deliberately falling backward into the Caribbean Sea. With a push on its valve, my buoyancy control vest inflated, and I adjusted the full-face mask that would permit radio communication with the surface craft. Around me, two freelance cameramen were discussing who would take the wide shot and who would come in close. Neither was enthusiastic about the latter. Because swimming about twenty-five feet below our fin tips were dozens of sharks.

This was another exciting, somewhat insane assignment given to me by the brilliant, somewhat insane executive producer of *Good Morning America*, Shelley Ross.

It was Shelley who sent me up in a Marchetti fighter plane for air-to-air combat using lasers for a story about extreme vacations. I managed to win the dogfight by pulling an Immelmann maneuver, going inverted after passing below my opponent and then leveling off as I came up behind him. I guess all those years of video game playing paid off.

It was Shelley who pitted me against our superstar anchor, Diane Sawyer, in a street luge race in Central Park. I still think the contest was rigged.

It was Shelley who gave me a week to train with free-dive experts for a go at breaking the American record for an unassisted (no weights) descent on a single breath of air. By the time of the attempt, I was holding my breath for over 3.5 minutes in the training pool. With cameramen in deep-sea diving suits stationed all along my route into the murky depths, I dove to 150 feet, a new record (but no longer), on live TV. When I surfaced, a safety diver made sure I wiped the blood and mucous from my face, residue of the sixty-six pounds per square inch of pressure my skull endured at that depth.

It was Shelley who chartered a luxurious jet for Robin Roberts and me to compete against each other's teams of viewers in a cross-country scavenger hunt she dubbed "The X-Treme Urban Challenge." We raced to find obscure street names, or solve riddles, or escape an actual prison, from Dallas to Boston to San Francisco. "Let's face it," Robin told a reporter, "It's all about the competition, going up against a pretty boy, Don Dahler, and kicking some butt." In the end, Robin's team squeaked out a win. But the highlight of the entire adventure was climbing into the chartered jet as soon as we got off the air and being served cocktails and gourmet food while speeding off to the next location. I can't even imagine what the entire escapade cost. But the ratings were great. Twenty years later, when Robin interviewed me about my book *Fearless*, we had a good laugh over the lunacy and fun of that outrageous assignment.

And it was Shelley who paid a fortune to send a team to the South China Sea island of Pulau Tiga in a tongue-in-cheek attempt to uncover which contestant won the first season of CBS's massive hit reality show *Survivor*. The competition was over, but the finale had yet to air. So, in addition to filming all the trash, empty water bottles, and mockups of crashed WWII fighter planes Mark Burnett's crew had carelessly left behind to spoil the idyllic scenery, we wandered around the resort at the other end of the island where the cast (once voted off) and crew lived in holiday splendor, showing photos of the final three contestants and asking the locals who was buying the most drinks and who seemed happiest. Yes, it was an unscientific survey. And, yes, we got it wrong. (I had guessed it was former Navy Seal Rudy Boesch.) We were so far south that the techs had to place our satellite dish, which was shipped in via a Chinese junk, at the farthest end of the only pier and point it directly at the horizon to hit the satellite. Just prior to our first live report from the island, our tech announced there was a 0.006 percent chance of actually getting our signal back to New York. Somehow, we did.

And now, Shelley Ross was literally feeding her national correspondent to the sharks. Stuart Cove, who ran the shark dive facility in the Bahamas where we were filming, floated over to check my gear. I had long ago achieved PADI expert diver certification, but the last thing Cove wanted was to lose a network reporter because of equipment failure.

"Ready?" he asked. I gave him a thumbs-up, and Stuart and I kicked down to where all the sharks were milling about. We settled down onto our knees next to the bait box. Three-to-nine-foot Caribbean reef sharks, a species responsible for most attacks on humans, wandered languidly around us, waiting for breakfast.

As I interviewed him over the radio masks, Stuart stabbed various large chunks of tuna he had in the bait box using a three-foot-long pole and held them out for the sharks to eat. I began doing the same. It was great TV, with sharks swimming up to the camera lenses and away, and Stuart and me just chatting about these amazing creatures, how most shark attacks are the result of mistaken identity—when suddenly one grabbed my arm and gave it a good yank. Luckily, we were wearing sleeves of chain mail on our "feeding" arms, so I wasn't injured. But then another big guy decided my leg looked more appetizing than the fish I was holding out to him and gave it a good chomp.

"That one just bit me," I declared, calmer than I had any right to be. I felt his teeth enter my calf, then spit it out. Yes, it hurt. Like a bad dog bite. But I played it off, hoping the water wasn't getting cloudy from my blood and that my blood wouldn't rile up all the other sharks.

The taping was quickly over, and we ascended to the surface and onto the boat without further incident.

As I pulled off my mask, I turned to the camera and said, "Man. I've never felt more like a McDonald's Happy Meal in my life."

CHAPTER 30

HANGING CHADS AND JET SKIS

I didn't do politics. The networks I worked for over the years always had plenty of other people more connected and knowledgeable about that than me. But when the 2000 presidential election came down to a legal battle in Florida, it was all hands on deck.

Unfortunately, the producers at *Good Morning America* decided at the last minute to add me to the ranks of staff members covering this historic event on the ground. Also unfortunately, by the time they sent me on my way south, the only hotel room available for fifty miles was the most expensive suite at Palm Beach's Four Seasons Resort. Darn. Ocean views. Gigantic bed. Minibar. Life can truly suck for a hardworking journalist such as myself.

Perhaps I should give you a brief refresher: George W. Bush and Al Gore were neck and neck on the night of November 7. It all came down to the Sunshine State's twenty-five Electoral College votes. The AP initially called the state for Gore, then reversed itself a few hours later, dubbing it "too close to call," then announced Bush had won, then reversed itself again and said it was still too close to call. Gore phoned Bush and conceded, then later retracted his concession after his staff informed him just how tight the count was. Hospital emergency rooms filled up with whiplash victims who'd made the mistake of trying to follow the bouncing ball. Bush's lead was 1,784—within the margin triggering an automatic machine recount under Florida law. That began the next morning. Bush's winning margin was quickly reduced to just 327 state-wide votes. The fate of the nation rested on about the number of people in an Applebee's on any given Thursday.

Gore's camp then requested a manual recount in four counties: Miami-Dade, Broward, Volusia, and Palm Beach. Bush's camp sued to stop it. A federal court ruled against them.

Florida's secretary of state, Katherine Harris, who was ultimately responsible for certification of the state's election results, also happened to moonlight as cochair of the Bush campaign in Florida. Move along. Nothing to see here. No conflict of interest whatsoever. Nope. Oh, and Bush's brother, Jeb, was the state's governor. Like I said, I didn't do politics. But that didn't mean I didn't pay attention. *Anyhoo....*

Thus began the weekslong circus of county election workers diligently scrutinizing the paper ballots to discern the will of the people. Terms such as *butterfly ballots* and *hanging chads* became the stuff of late-night commentary. Newspapers featured photos of officials holding ballots up to the light and peering at them as if they held the secret to fusion reaction.

One of those officials was a man I interviewed years earlier for an unrelated story. I'm going to withhold his name so as not to subject him to any legal or extremist repercussions. But he would be instantly recognizable to anyone who watched the news back then. Let's call him Stan. The day after I arrived and checked in to my disgustingly palatial hovel, I was walking across the parking lot next to the administrative building hosting the recount when I heard someone shout my name. It was Stan. We chatted for a moment, and he offered me his personal cell phone number. "Call me if you have any questions," he said, before pushing through the maelstrom of reporters who had descended on us and were thrusting microphones in his face.

So here's a little suggestion for everyone, not just journalists: treat people fairly and honestly because you should.
Virtue is its own reward. But sometimes there is also a karmic
reward for doing so. I had just received mine.

That evening I called Stan, and he gave me a complete
rundown of what had occurred in the recount room. The next
morning on *GMA* I reported such, with details no one else
had. That began a daily routine. I would update the audience
first thing in the morning, call Stan later that night, and relay
his information the next morning. One day in particular, after
I tossed back to Diane Sawyer, and she threw the show into
a commercial break, she offhandedly asked me if I knew of
an official who could answer a question she had right then.
I glanced across the parking lot, spotted Stan in the midst of
a gaggle of cameras and reporters, and told her, "Just a minute." I walked over, pushed through the crowd, whispered a
few words in his ear, and led Stan back to talk to Diane, not
realizing that it was all broadcast live on CNN. Out of the
break, Diane had a nice chat with Stan. But I had more than
a few apologies to make with the other TV crews over drinks
that night.

The Palm Beach recount was of particular interest due to
its newly designed ballots, which managed to thoroughly con-
fuse voters enough that thousands of them erroneously voted
for Reform Party candidate Pat Buchanan. Ultimately, 19,000
such ballots were "spoiled," meaning voters realized their mistake and voted a second time on the same paper, invalidat-
ing the ballot. A 2001 study by the *American Political Science
Review* determined that faulty design cost Al Gore the election.

I was up, dressed, and camera ready at 6:00 a.m. every
morning. There was no video to shoot, no one else to interview, no actual piece to put together—I simply stood before
the camera and repeated what Stan had told me, attributing
the information to "an election official." The producers back in
New York were ecstatic. ABC's actual political reporters were

grateful for the inside scoop. And I ended up having hours and hours of free time in the middle of the day, in southern Florida, in November, on an expense account.

I developed an impressive tan and was on a first-name basis with the resort's tennis pros. I tried out every amazing restaurant in a five-mile radius. Olympic gold-medalist swimmer Dara Torres, whom I'd come to know through interviews over the past year, was vacationing nearby. We met a few times on the beach or at a restaurant to catch up on life. Earlier that summer, she'd been awarded five more medals in Sydney and was sporting a nifty little Olympic rings tattoo in a discrete location. Don't read anything into that—we were just friends.

Because of my windfall of daily information, the *GMA* producer assigned to work with me, John Green, also had some free time; although, given his other responsibilities, he had much less than me. We took to renting jet skis to ride out on the Intracoastal Waterway, jumping boat wakes and racing at full throttle. It was, all in all, some of the most fun I've ever had on assignment.

But, alas, all good things come to an end. On December 12, the Republican-leaning US Supreme Court handed down a ruling that effectively ended the recount and awarded the presidency to George W. Bush. Oddly, the majority instructed that its judgment should not set a precedent but rather be "limited to the present circumstances." I'll refrain from comment on that one.

The next day I packed up my bathing suit, tennis shoes, and suntan and departed for the cold Northeast. I called Stan one last time from the airport to thank him. He was sincerely pleased to have made the recount's work a little more transparent, no matter how messy the process. "You did the American public a great service," I told him. "None of this should ever be done in secret." I promised to buy him dinner the next time he came to New York.

It took three days to go through all my receipts and submit the expense report. ABC's bean counters were not happy.

CHAPTER 31

HELL ON EARTH

The day the world changed I awoke from a sleep troubled by forces outside my control. Economic ones. I was being laid off. My bosses at ABC News informed me weeks earlier that, since my contract was coming up and they faced mandatory cutbacks, I held the short stick. It was nothing personal, they insisted, and my work was respected, and they really, really didn't want to lose me, but numbers were numbers. In a fit of corporate downsizing, ABC's parent company, Disney, handed down the law that only a very few contracts in the news division could be renewed, and mine was not one of them.

I had one week to go before I was to clean out my office. It was, needless to say, not a good morning. Before then I'd only been fired one other time, while working my way through college as a bartender. I heard one thing from a cocktail waitress, but the customer had ordered something different. The customer happened to be the short-tempered bar owner. End of job.

So here I was, after climbing to a new pinnacle in my career and finally getting to work on ABC's vaunted news magazine shows, I was told I would no longer be needed. Suddenly, I had new empathy for dot-com executives and auto workers who'd faced the pink slips during the recent recession, the men and women whose turn of luck I'd reported on. It was like one long drawn-out punch in the stomach.

Katie, my girlfriend at the time, sensing my darkened mood throughout the night, was already up and quietly clacking away at her computer in our Tribeca loft. She often worked from home as a corporate education consultant. That morning, not even the lovely sight of her padding across the loft still dressed in a T-shirt, coffee cup in hand and blonde hair twisted over one shoulder, could lift my spirits. There's a first time for everything, I guess.

A little more than a year earlier I spotted her at the Delta Shuttle waiting area at Reagan National Airport in Washington, DC. I was early for my scheduled flight back to New York, as usual, so I sat reading *USA Today* with a cup of lukewarm coffee. Even though there were shuttles to LaGuardia every half hour, I felt no need to get on one of the earlier ones. Until, that is, this petite, head-turning beauty stepped away from the ticket counter and walked past me to board the next outgoing plane. Her eyes met mine for just a smidgeon too long.

Life in those days for me was one of constant travel interspersed with all the wonderful trappings a single person can enjoy in Manhattan. I was dating an assortment of marvelous women, with no thoughts of marriage or children. "Happy and content" pretty much summed up my state of mind.

But as she swept by my seat, I caught a whiff of her subtle perfume. Somewhere deep in my chest, a bell sounded. One one thousand, two one thousand, three one thousand.... It took me all of ten seconds to say, "What the hell," go back up to the counter, and change my ticket for that flight.

Yes. I had become a bona fide stalker.

The shuttle had no assigned seating, so as I made my way down the aisle, I saw she had an entire row to herself on the left. "Excuse me," I said, "but you wouldn't happen to be Lisa Edwards, would you?" (That was the name of my high school crush. Hey, cut me a little slack—I was having to improvise on a dime.)

She smiled politely. "No."

"Oh. Well, you look just like her. Haven't seen her in ages. Is anyone sitting there?" I motioned to the seat next to her.

Another smile. "No."

I slipped by her and settled into the window seat. Preflight song and dance by the flight attendants. Taxing on the runway. Waiting in a long line of other jets. Take off. Drinks and snacks.

"So what *is* your name," I finally asked.

"Katie."

I extended a hand. "I'm Don. Nice to meet you." I'm pretty sure I caught sight of an eye roll from the woman seated across the aisle from us.

We chatted for the rest of the short flight. I found out she had a PhD in linguistics from Georgetown, was an athlete in college, came from one of the nation's founding families, and was coxswain on Oxford's winning eights rowing team during her junior year abroad. So, yeah, all that and cute as hell, too.

By the time we landed, I was toast. She moved into my place a few months later.

The morning of September 11, I roused from bed later than usual and poured myself a cup, mumbling an attempt at a civil greeting. I had a late edit on a *Nightline* piece scheduled for that evening, so there was no reason to head uptown to the ABC facility on Sixty-Sixth Street at my normal time. As it would likely be my last piece for the network, I was in no hurry to finish it. Any other day I would've already been in the office.

Our loft at the corner of Church and Duane was one large room on the third floor of a converted warehouse, considered classic and trendy now, but not too many years before I found the place, it was a marginal living space for artists who could afford little else. Living room, kitchen, office, and bedroom took up all points of the compass in a perfectly square space. Eighteen-foot ceilings, exposed brick, and hardwood floors somehow made it seem more spacious than a typical cookie-cutter New York City apartment. The only interior wall closed off the tiny bathroom. As a result, my walk that morning from covers to coffee maker took me through no doorways. I was headed to the couch with a mug of Starbucks Kenya AA when the sound split the air.

It was like an enormous ripping of fabric, a shriek and deep roar all at once, followed by a huge explosion. It was a sound similar to one I'd heard before, but only in countries at war. Never in the US, and certainly not in lower Manhattan.

"That's a missile," I said aloud, not believing it even as I said it, but my mind at that moment couldn't find any other reference for that specific sound.

Understandably, Katie scoffed. "No, that's just a truck or something." One of the unfortunate realities of living in downtown New York City was the constant loud bangs of trucks passing over those temporary metal plates on the streets or garbage trucks dropping huge bins back to the sidewalk. I knew this wasn't that.

By the time she finished that sentence, I'd made it to the window above Church Street and looked up. A massive fireball billowed out of the side of the North Tower. I heard screams on the street below.

"They've hit the World Trade Center," I said. Looking into the maw a thousand feet up, I could see giant flames continuing to gout out. The interior of the hole was dark, but through the smoke and flames some of the building's enormous steel support beams were visible.

I spun around and began searching for the cordless phone. It never seemed to be in its recharging cradle. The clock next to the bed read 8:49.

Our television stood to the right of the windows, and it seemed mere seconds before Charlie Gibson and Diane

Sawyer on *Good Morning America* were saying something about reports of a small plane hitting the World Trade Center. I finally located the phone's handset and dialed the *GMA* control room, a number I knew by heart through years of early morning conversations with the show's producers while on assignment for them in one place or another.

Melissa Thomas, a bright and extremely competent young producer, answered. I quickly told her I was just a few blocks away from the WTC and was looking right at the burning building. Without hesitation, Melissa shouted, "Phoner! Dahler's on line six at the scene!" and within minutes my voice was patched in live to the studio, where I tried to put into words what I was seeing.

Diane Sawyer: "Don, where are you and what do you know?"

"I'm about four or five blocks just north of the World Trade Center. About ten minutes ago there was a loud sound—I can only describe that it sounded like a missile, not an airplane. Then there was a loud explosion and immediately lots of screaming out on the streets. I don't want to cause any speculation, but that's the only way I can describe the sound. The sound itself was not a prop plane. It was perhaps a jet, but it could have been a missile as well. You can see quite a lot of damage. If it was an airplane it had to be huge."

As Diane and Charlie Gibson calmly continued asking me questions, I remember distinctly thinking that I, too, had to remain professional and, above all, accurate. I realized I was, at that moment, a radio reporter, since I had no live camera with me. It was crucial to describe the scene in as detailed a fashion as I could without embellishing in any way. Edward R. Murrow's riveting dispatches from the rooftops of London during the Battle of Britain in World War II flashed in my mind. He became my role model that morning.

There were things I witnessed that day—such as the horrific images of people choosing to throw themselves out of the window rather than die painfully in the flames—that I deliberately did not mention on live television. Because I simply couldn't confirm that's what was actually happening. Deep down I also knew there were loved ones watching the tragedy unfold, and I didn't want to cause them more torture than they were already experiencing.

The smoke at the top of the massive buildings grew thicker. Emergency vehicles were converging from every direction, their sirens wailing. I reiterated that what I'd heard could very well have been a jet, but with the damage to the building relative to its sheer size as a city block wide, it would have to have been a large jet.

After discussions with Diane about how close the various airports are to lower Manhattan and how planes often fly nearby, Charlie asked me to describe what I was seeing now.

"There appears to be more and more fire and smoke enveloping the very top of the building. As fire crews are descending on this area, it does not appear that there's any kind of effort up there…"

That was the exact moment when the second plane wheeled into the South Tower. Viewers and the anchors watching on their TVs all saw it happen live. From my vantage point all I could see was an enormous explosion one hundred stories off the ground.

> Me: "Now remember—OH MY GOD!"
>
> Diane (almost under her breath): "Oh my god…"
>
> Charlie: "That looks like a second plane has just hit…"
>
> Me: "I did not see a plane go in. That just exploded."

Charlie continued, realizing I didn't have the benefit of the live television feeds they were watching, patiently explaining,

"We just saw another plane coming in from the side. So this looks like some sort of concerted effort to attack the World Trade Center is underway in downtown New York."

I was as stunned as anyone. Up until that second I'd assumed that if it had been a commercial jet that hit the North Tower, it was some sort of terrible mistake. An equipment failure or pilot error. As Charlie Gibson so matter-of-factly stated, the second attack left no doubt.

At about 9:14, Peter Jennings and terrorism expert John Miller took over anchor duties from the ABC News main studio. The towers continued to burn. My cordless phone battery was dying, so I traded it for our second one and climbed out onto the fire escape. Looking down, I saw what appeared to be a large jet engine lying on top of a partially collapsed bus stop not half a block away.

Peter talked to a number of eyewitnesses and aviation expert John Nance about what kind of jets these might have been.

Around 9:40 another plane struck, this time the Pentagon. The network shifted its focus to that emerging story.

About half an hour later I was still on the fire escape, waiting on the line in case Peter had any questions, when I felt the earth shake and heard an enormous rumble. The top of one of the towers seemed to shimmy, and then plumes of smoke and debris began to fall. Beneath my feet I could feel a rhythmic pounding as each floor of the South Tower collapsed on the next.

The ever-unflappable Peter Jennings interrupted correspondent Pierre Thomas talking about the Pentagon to try to describe what was now happening in New York, but words failed him. "Let's go to the Trade tower now because, John, we now have a...what do we have?"

After a few moments of Peter and John Miller trying to surmise what they were seeing on their television monitor, they came to me. "Dan Dahler from ABC's *Good Morning*

America is down in the general vicinity. Dan, can you tell us what just happened?"

In Peter's defense, I hadn't done much reporting for his broadcast up to that point, and he probably didn't bother to watch much of the morning show. I quickly corrected him for the record before moving on.

"Yes, Peter, it's Don Dahler here. I'm four blocks north of the World Trade Center. The second building that was hit by a plane has just completely collapsed. The entire building has just collapsed as if a demolition team set it off, when you see the demolitions of old buildings. It folded down on itself, and it's not there anymore."

Peter was incredulous. "The whole side has collapsed?"

"The whole building has collapsed."

He let out an audible gasp, struggling as we all did with the enormity of that moment. And the undeniably horrendous loss of life we were all witnessing.

I dove back into the apartment and quickly shut the window just as an enormous cloud of smoke and dust and debris rolled up Church Street, covering everyone and everything in a fine white powder. When it finally passed, crowds of people still fleeing northward stumbled along, like zombies, wiping their eyes, grabbing bottles of water to try to clear the dust from their noses and mouths.

Almost exactly thirty minutes later, shortly after John Miller announced that the emergency triage center downtown was being relocated to a nearby high school due to concerns over the structural integrity of the North Tower, that tower too collapsed.

All cell service ceased the instant the second tower fell because of the loss of all the radio antennae on its roof. Electrical power was cut as well. But I was able to continue reporting via my cordless phone until its battery finally gave out. When live trucks and other correspondents finally made it down to the scene, I left my building and wandered down to the newly erected police barricades, where I was summarily stopped from going closer. Our NYPD-issued press credentials clearly state journalists have the right to cross police lines wherever formed—except, evidently, in cases of terrorism.

Then I heard my name being called. I looked past the barrier to see a face from the not-so-distant past—an FBI source who'd helped me on some investigations. I've never revealed his name and never will. He had escaped from the bureau's offices in Building Seven shortly before the towers collapsed. We chatted for a moment, and then he said, "Would you like to go in?"

"Of course."

"Then come with me. No cameras, no pictures."

"OK."

He showed his badge to clear me past the police line, and we walked a few debris-covered blocks to where the two towers once stood. It was, to say the least, hell on earth. A thick, choking dust hovered in the air. Numerous fires were still burning amid gigantic pieces of the buildings, which appeared to have been jammed into the earth by the force of the collapse. There were bodies and even more gruesome carnage scattered everywhere. The incessant beeping of emergency responder beacons seemed to be coming from all around us. Hundreds of rescuers were gathered into groups, many crying in frustration because their superiors had not yet determined if it was safe enough for them to begin searching for survivors in the rubble. I witnessed thousands, perhaps millions, of sheets of paper still fluttering down. Picking one up from the ground, I saw it was partially singed, an earnings report from the financial services firm Cantor Fitzgerald.

I'm told I was the first network correspondent on the air from the scene earlier that morning, explaining to a stunned nation that their eyes weren't lying to them. I don't know if that's true, and it doesn't much matter. I didn't watch television, or listen to a radio, or even read a newspaper for days. There was too much work to do. That was the beginning of two weeks of straight around-the-clock coverage of the most important story of our lives. At some point, when I was about to go on the air for one of those broadcasts, ABC News president David Westin informed me they had renewed my contract.

In the days that followed, I stayed downtown, afraid to leave the area because the NYPD wasn't letting people come back in, even credentialed press. I took naps in my apartment that was without power or phones and worked a story that became all consuming. Katie finally relented and relocated uptown to keep working and have a healthier place to live. But not before we held each other on our couch and wept.

What stands out in my memory about those weeks are the voices and the faces behind them. The police K-9 rescue team who jumped in their truck moments after the first plane hit and drove nonstop from Illinois. I met them at 3:30 a.m. Wednesday morning as John and Dale lay on a restaurant's stoop, catching a few hours of sleep. Tucked under Dale's beefy arm, her chest rising in silent harmony with her handler's snores, was Miranda, their German Shepherd search dog. The men were gruff spoken and shy, and you loved them for that. They worked fifteen-hour shifts, and by the time they reluctantly packed up their truck and left for home four days later, Miranda's paws were shredded from the hot, ragged metal she'd been climbing over. After that first night they'd moved from their sidewalk beds to the floor of my apartment, refusing to dirty the couch or bed, but since we were basically working opposite shifts, I never got to know them much better than my first impression. And my first impression was that these were the kind of men who make America truly great.

Then there was the resident surgeon who'd just gotten to New York on vacation early that Tuesday and watched the events of September 11 unfold, like the rest of the world, on television. When Mayor Rudolph Giuliani went on local TV to ask for help from medical personnel, he hopped in the cab, not bothering to change, since, like most medical students, he slept in a bootleg set of scrubs. An hour later he found himself perched on a metal beam over a bottomless chasm, working to keep alive a Port Authority cop whose leg was trapped between two steel support columns. While stabilizing the cop's vital signs, he chatted with him, and prayed with him, and secretly hoped he'd be able to save the guy's leg. He did. And when I interviewed him as he wearily walked up Church Street to catch a cab back to his hotel, all he could talk about was how amazed he was at the bravery of the firemen who had been working all around him.

Throughout the days that followed, I made numerous trips to ground zero, my neighborhood, usually as a journalist, sometimes as a volunteer, working on the pile with a thousand others, digging by hand so as not to further injure any survivors we came across. Sadly, I never came across any. Due to police restrictions on cameras at the site, I often had to rely simply on words the next morning to describe to millions of viewers what was happening at the place where their friends, loved ones, coworkers, and fellow Americans (as well as people from 101 other nations) had vanished from our world. I interviewed rescuers who awed me with their humility and determination, and searchers who tore my heart with their pleas for help, all the while denying a fading belief that they'd ever find the husband or mother whose face was on that piece of paper. They held back their desperation with sheer, steely strength, but it shone in their eyes, and their eyes haunt me still. Their eyes said, Tell me you saw this person walking around, or in a hospital, or being interviewed, or sitting dazed by the street. Please tell me you saw this person alive. The fact that I could never once answer yes is why I can never forget that question.

One last memory of that terrible day. Before the first tower collapsed, there was a period of time when the network was consumed with what was happening at the Pentagon. They weren't coming to me much anymore for reports. So I decided that was my opportunity to get closer to the rescue attempts.

I knew some of the firemen who worked Engine 7/Ladder 1 on our block and figured I could link up with them and videotape them going into the towers. I opened the drawer that holds all my camera gear and electronics to grab my camcorder. But it wasn't there. I looked around the apartment, but to no avail. Reluctantly, I had to abandon that plan.

Anyone who knows me knows I have a thing about always putting stuff back where it goes. I'm practically anal about it. And, in fact, a few days later I opened that drawer again. And there it was. The camcorder, sitting right on top.

Had I found it on September 11, I would not be telling you this now.

And Katie and I would not have gotten married the following spring.

CHAPTER 32

MOMENT OF TROTH

Diane Sawyer was having a blast. Every time the director switched to me on *Good Morning America*, she would refer to the countdown clock in the corner of the screen with a twinkle in her eye and tease me about what was about to happen.

It was Katie's and my wedding day, March 22, 2002. Katie was at home, getting ready for our small, intimate ceremony that was to take place at the Central Park Boathouse at 10:30 that morning, and I was in the Times Square studio filling in as the morning show's newsreader. It seemed strange, in retrospect, that Shelley Ross, *GMA*'s executive producer, and Diane insisted there was no one else available for the job that morning and that I'd be finished in plenty of time to make it to the "church" on time—strange, that is, until I began reading the national forecast in my first segment, and it included the temperatures for Katie, Oklahoma; Donald, Oregon; Groom, Texas; and Bridal Veil Falls, California. What followed was a series of very sweet, funny, sometimes awkward, but always warm moments of affection manufactured by the special people with whom I'd worked for so long.

Robin Roberts and George Stephanopoulos, the latter a newlywed himself, happily offered advice and mercilessly ribbed me as Diane handed out "something old, something new" gifts. I cracked jokes and told the story of how we met while trying hard not to show how moved and, frankly, embarrassed I was by their attentions. My one and only regret was that my mom hadn't lived long enough to see the spectacle. She would have loved it. She passed away suddenly from a pulmonary embolism right before I accepted the position with ABC News.

Katie, ever the gamer, handled it beautifully, but I knew for a fact that national network coverage of our nuptials was not something she'd ever imagined.

As the broadcast ended I was celebrated with a shower of rice by the fans waiting on the street before ducking into a car and heading uptown.

One thing we hadn't planned on when picking that particular date was a late spring frost. The temperature in Central Park was twenty-four degrees, with constant, chilly gusts. As our dear friend David Murray somehow managed to take lovely photographs of the beautiful bride next to the lake despite the frigid weather, the staff of the Loeb Boathouse scrambled to move the flowers, chairs, and tables into a vacant corner of the popular restaurant. There, with but a handful of our closest friends and family members, we exchanged vows and declared, "I do."

Just as the ceremony began, a sparrow flew down and alighted on the floor between Katie and me. The tiny bird stood watching, turning ever so slightly as one or the other of us spoke.

As we kissed for the first time as husband and wife, the sparrow fluttered up to the ceiling and then out an open window.

My brother, Erik, leaned over and said, "You knew Mom wasn't going to miss this."

CHAPTER 33

TIME TRAVEL

The explosion ripped my legs from my body and blinded me. I could hear an airplane approaching, strafing our position with its machine guns, but I couldn't run. I couldn't do anything. I lay there, waiting to die. Then another explosion shook me awake. Only it wasn't an explosion. It was turbulence.

I looked around me, confused. It took a few moments to realize it was another nightmare. I'd had them on a regular basis for the past two weeks, a residual effect of the Trade Center attacks. Sometimes I was caught inside the enormous rolling cloud of choking dust and debris I couldn't escape. Sometimes I was on one of the top floors of the buildings, looking out into open air, feeling the flames at my back. This particular bad dream was a new one, a dark premonition from my subconscious, perhaps, preparing itself for yet another war.

The Soviet-era Tajikistan Airlines Antonov-72 was only a quarter full. Most of us on board were reporters and photographers, stuffed into tiny, cramped, hard-as-church-pews seats, on our way to Afghanistan. We almost didn't make it off the ground. Between all the big cases of camera and satellite equipment, personal gear, and supplies, the ancient plane was dangerously overweight. After lots of yelling and gesturing among themselves, the flight crew ordered us to remove the dozens of cases of bottled water. Finally satisfied, they closed the cabin door and started the enormous twin engines that sat on top of the wings like shoulder pads on a football player. We departed London at 4:00 a.m.

Five hours later, the AN-72 landed in Trabzon, Turkey, for refueling. We were ordered to disembark and wait in a vast, empty terminal under heavy guard. Westerners, it seemed, were not exactly welcome there. A kindly airport employee appeared with the key to the duty-free area, and we had just enough time for a much-needed coffee before we were herded back on board for the remainder of the twelve-hour flight.

At 9:15 a.m. we could see Dushanbe, the capital of Tajikistan, as we approached the airport. It took two hours for our local fixer, Tomak, to sort things out with the government bureaucrats while we waited on the tarmac, but finally we made it out of the airport and to our hotel. My ABC team, producers Bruno Roeber and Nick Watt, cameraman Bartley Price, and soundman Joao Valle, found a nearby restaurant where we feasted on tomato salad, dumpling soup, cheese pie, meat pie, chicken skewers, and plenty of beer and vodka, in anticipation of a dry couple of months in a nation where alcohol was illegal. We danced with each other, the restaurant staff, and any passersby who decided to join the party.

This was my second trip to Dushanbe. The city always struck me as somewhat bipolar, with block after block of depressing, decaying concrete buildings constructed during Stalin's regime, dissected by the occasional lush, tree-lined avenues of museums, embassies, and the impressive presidential palace.

After a good night's sleep, we were up and packed and waiting in line back at the airport, along with a dozen other journalists, to get our permits, visas stamped, and tickets for the short helicopter ride into Afghanistan. Midway through the morning, an official came out to announce there would be no flights that day. And, it turned out, none the next, as well.

Finally, on October 2, our small horde of reporters and technicians were allowed onto the military base and directed to a corner of the runway where sat two large Russian helicopters, relics of the Cold War. Upon close inspection, I could see bullet holes in the side of one of them, still dripping what appeared to be motor oil. Interesting bit of trivia: more war correspondents are killed coming and going to their assignments than by bullets or bombs. I've had more cliffside close calls in rickety buses and near-tragic traffic accidents in various taxis and rental cars en route to a story than I care to remember. A jetliner I was once in pulled up suddenly while on approach to a landing in Chad because a tank sat in the middle of the runway, its turret pointed our way. "There appears to be a coup underway," the pilot calmly announced over the intercom. "We are being diverted to Nigeria." The job of a traveling correspondent is anything but glamorous.

There was a bit of a chaotic scramble among the journalists to get all the gear loaded, which pissed off the Afghani organizers who made everyone disembark and wait in the boiling sun until they could add up how much everything weighed. Once we were back on board, the enormous rotors began turning, and the pilots gave it a practice hop about twenty feet up and back down, to see if there was still too big a load. Evidently it was acceptable, because we were soon flying low above villages and green fields. Forty minutes later we crossed over the Panj River, which marks the border between the two countries. We landed in a field outside the northern Afghan town of Khoja Bahauddin.

The philosopher René Descartes described *travel* as talking with men from other centuries. In no place is that truer than in Khoja. This region is straight out of Biblical times, constructed of mud and straw huts, where young boys herd donkeys laden with hay, jokingly called "Afghan motorcycles" by the locals, fully veiled women draw water from wells using crude pulleys and ropes, and a town crier wanders around, giving the news of the day.

ABC's Moscow bureau chief, Mike Lee, was in the process of setting up the compound we would share with CBS, and it was a thing of wonder. Mike was the guy who hit the ground ahead of everyone else, figured out who ran things and how to get them done, arranged for vehicles, drivers, translators, and security. He always reminded me of Kurtz, from Joseph Conrad's "Heart of Darkness," who was preternaturally comfortable venturing into unknown territory. Except Mike was thankfully calm, sane, and humble, as opposed to Kurtz's "going crazy and demanding to be worshiped" minor peccadillos.

When we hiked the half mile or so from the landing site to the compound, one of many dust storms that would vex us the entire time there was kicking up. Mike's army of workers were busy adding porches to the second story and roof of the main building to be used as live-shot platforms, digging a latrine, and finishing up the mud brick wall that surrounded the place. An armed guard stood at the entrance. As tensions in the area increased over time, security was beefed up. Journalists are always juicy targets.

We spent the rest of the day setting up our own living quarters, which in my case was a small, nylon tent next to the pit where workers used manure, mud, and straw to make bricks. *Location, location, location.* I had picked a doozy of a site. Some days the odor was overwhelming. Thanks to the hot wind that stirred up the arid ground, everything in my tent was immediately coated with a fine, talcum-like coating. Most of us developed upper respiratory tract infections over the next few weeks as a result.

Alcohol was technically forbidden in that Islamic country, but Mike managed to smuggle quite a few bottles in. Hey, before you judge, it was extraordinarily difficult and dangerous work. I don't think an occasional glass or two of whiskey angered Allah. He had other things to fret about in that region. As we gratefully washed the grit from our throats, he gave us the rundown of operations, from the crucial to the mundane. We would be sharing a satellite dish with CBS, so we had to coordinate our video feeds and live-shot times. Travel anywhere must be cleared first by the local officials. Gasoline was trucked in overland, a five-day-long, dangerous journey, and thus cost twenty dollars a gallon. And while using the latrine, one should lean a designated stick across the entrance to warn others away, as there was no door. Mike had big plans to build a second, ladies-only bathroom with gravity-fed showers.

Speaking of the latrine, toilet paper was a rare commodity, so paper of any kind for that sanitary purpose was in high demand. Every magazine, newspaper, and discarded book was fair game. Or one could simply handle things the way Muslims and Hindus have for centuries, with water and one's left hand doing the, ahem, dirty work (never your right—that is for handling food and so on).

Not everyone made an immediate adjustment. A newly arrived reporter for a local New York affiliate—who shall remain nameless—found himself in dire straits one morning, so he pulled some Afghani bills from his pocket to use to wipe his nether region. Unfortunately, one of the Afghan guards spotted the colorful currency floating among the sewage and raised a stink (my sincere apologies). The entire camp of workers took offense, so Mike had to issue an edict that money was not to be used as toilet paper. The next day, one of the cameramen saw the reporter on the way to the latrine again and loudly asked him if he needed change for a ten.

With post–9/11 interest in Afghanistan at a high among viewers, we began getting on the air almost immediately. At first our "hits," as we call them, took the form of simple on-camera debriefs, describing the political and military situations, with a little history thrown in. But gradually, after befriending the deputy foreign minister, who went by his last name only,

Zubair, we were able to venture into a nearby refugee camp. The piece we shot there was about a man who escaped his village when the Taliban arrived and insisted every male had to take up arms and fight for them. He told us he saw old men murdered if they refused. As with many of his fellow villagers, the man said he promised to take up arms against the Northern Alliance, only to flee with his family in the middle of the night. As we watched, he said goodbye to his wife and children and climbed into the back of a pickup truck, heading to the front lines to fight—not with the Taliban but against them.

Unfortunately, that piece never aired. Someone back in New York questioned whether the man's account was real or apocryphal. There's always one of those dummies in every newsroom, the know-it-all who has never set foot in a war zone but doesn't trust the people who are actually on the ground.

It took patience and countless cups of tea, but finally producer Nick Watt (who eventually became a terrific correspondent for CNN) and I convinced Zubair to let us go to the front. He had his assistant draw up a letter of introduction, and we were off the next morning in two four-wheel-drive vehicles, mandatory in this rugged region: a Toyota double-cab pickup and a Russian-made UAZ, a Jeep-knockoff derisively called the "butting goat" throughout Central Asia for its stiff springs and brutally bumpy ride.

Traveling over miles of rutted dirt roads, past ancient villages with craftsmen and farmers doing exactly what they've done for centuries, it's easy to imagine Alexander the Great's vast army marching in the shadow of these stark, jagged mountains in the year 329 BC, or Genghis Khan in AD 1221, or the British in 1841, or the Soviets in 1979, and the soldiers wondering, Why the hell would anyone want to conquer this desolate place? Afghanistan truly is the graveyard of empires. Every invading army has realized that—to their peril. While finally giving up and trying to retreat over the Khyber Pass, the British garrison of sixteen thousand was totally wiped out, with only a single soldier surviving. The Soviet Union lost 115,000 troops in its ten-year-long attempt to create a vassal state. This is a land and a people that have known little other than war and death and poverty for thousands of years.

The reminders of conflict are everywhere: burned-out tanks and other military vehicles, abandoned artillery and rocket launchers, the ground still littered with thousands of empty shell casings. But most disconcertingly for us were the estimated six million working landmines still buried along roadways and walking paths throughout the north. A study by the United Nations reports that 46,868 Afghans have died since 1989 from stepping on or driving over those explosives. Two-thirds of the victims were children. In every village through which we passed, we could see men hobbling about on crutches, missing at least one limb. All of this made the moments when we were forced to swerve around large potholes and off the established road that much more interesting.

Bartley Price, an NFL-tight-end-sized Kiwi cameraman whose multilingual command of every known and unknown curse word was legendary, and his gregarious Brazilian soundman Joao Valle, whose affable calm was the polar opposite of his coworker, bounced around in the back seats of the Toyota. I had developed a lovely multi colored bruise on my right shoulder from continuously slamming against the door. As the miles slowly ticked up on the odometer, the tires sloughed through dust deep enough to leave a wake. There weren't many vehicles not pulled by livestock that came this way. We were following a tattered paper map, as GPS guidance for nonmilitary types like us didn't yet exist. One or both of the vehicles broke down on a regular basis. Most of the time I could get them running by simply scraping out the clogged fuel filters with a screwdriver or sacrificing our drinking water to keep the radiators full.

But the scenes we witnessed along the way were memorable and lovely, as noted in my journal:

> Men, beside a ten-foot-high pile of wheat, tossing pitchfork-fulls into the air for the wind to separate the grain from the chaff. Two young women, fully encased in bright white burkas, astride a donkey, with only their eyes visible through the lattice of their veils. An artisan working beside the road, hammering kitchen pots out of large artillery shell casings. And children, beautiful children, some with blue or green eyes, constantly running alongside our vehicles, laughing and talking and fearlessly curious.

After hours of arduous driving, we reached the first checkpoint for the Northern Alliance, the loose affiliation of warlords and militias who found common cause against the Taliban, whom they viewed as foreign invaders. We sat and broke bread with their commander, who declared we'd have to see a higher-ranking commander named Ishmat down the road.

The drive to their headquarters didn't take long, and the commander took our letter of introduction from Zubair and studied it closely. Ishmat was a middle-aged, fierce-looking man with, of course, a thick silvery beard. No adult men dared shave off their facial hair in Afghanistan, so all of us on the ABC team were attempting to sprout our own luxurious beards to fit in, with varying degrees of success. Mine was coming in somewhat patchy, like a cricket pitch on rocky ground. Bartley, gifted with a natural overabundance of testosterone, could've passed for a local. Joao's clung to the lower half of his face like a marmot hanging onto a cliff. And Nick—well, Nick looked like an erudite, manner-born, well-groomed male model no matter how long between trims. Damn him.

After we dined on tea, bread, and dates, the Afghan commander drew a crude map in the dirt as we knelt beside him. "Taliban," he said, pointing to a row of rectangles representing buildings. He shook his finger in the universal message of "no good."

Our translator relayed the rest of the message: the Taliban were much too entrenched in that particular area. They would undoubtedly shoot at us with artillery as soon as we appeared.

Ishmat then pointed to some other squares drawn on the ground and said, "Zard Kamar." "Much safer village," our translator explained. "No rockets. Not as many Taliban. But still a lot of fighting. Still dangerous."

Ishmat shook his head and murmured something in Dari. The translator responded. Then Ishmat shrugged and clapped his hands together, signifying the discussion was over. Later, the translator explained that the commander had asked, Why in the world would these Americans want to go there?

"What did you say?" I asked. He smiled, somewhat awkwardly, and said, "I told him you were crazy."

An hour more of driving and we arrived at the bank of a river. It was too deep for the UAZ to cross, so we all packed into the Toyota as a young boy on horseback, an enterprising fellow whose job was evidently to ferry locals across for a few coins, led the way through the shallowest part to the opposite side. The little Japanese truck left a black trail of oil in the water.

Up a steep bank, through a deep pit of muddy water—which somehow didn't flood the truck's engine—and over an extremely narrow mountain pass barely wide enough for the Toyota, and we found ourselves halted at yet another military checkpoint. The message was clearly relayed: from this point on, you're on foot. As we shrugged on our backpacks, our translator sheepishly approached me. "The man, he say you must wear a hat. Or Taliban will think you're Russian." He pointed at my sun-bleached hair. "They will kill you first."

That seemed reasonably good advice. I dug around in my pack and found a baseball cap.

About an hour into the hike, along a narrow, rocky path, we happened upon a group of Northern Alliance soldiers who were taking a break from the battle to catch a few hours of sleep or a meal or just pass around a cigarette. That's where I found the little owl I wrote about earlier, tethered to the ground and suffering from a gunshot wound to its wing. But that's also where I found a handful of soldiers, none of whom were older than seventeen. The youngest was fourteen.

So here's the thing about war that people in the so-called civilized world have a hard time grasping: there is a crucial difference between politically motivated military confrontations, like the US invasion of Grenada, and *existential* warfare, when your land and loved ones and future are at risk of ceasing to exist. That's the reality Ukraine faces as I write this. That's what Afghanistan has faced for countless generations. These days, we in America have an age requirement for citizens wishing to join the US military without parental consent—eighteen. But in past wars, the War for Independence, the Indian Wars, the War of 1812, and the Civil War, children fought and suffered and died alongside adults. Because everything they had and everything they loved and everything they aspired to be was on the line. Such was the present, past, and future facing the four young men I stood before, men who could barely produce peach fuzz on their chins,

They told me about the Taliban, how they took everything good in life away: the music, the art, the schools, the joy. They told me about friends and family members who disappeared in the night or were shot or hanged or mutilated for minor offenses. And they all used the same term to describe their enemy: *invaders.*

The first casualty of war might well be the truth, as US senator Hiram Johnson declared in 1918. But the second is innocence. I've seen boy soldiers in wars from Kosovo to

Africa. We witnessed a ceremony in Afghanistan where a newborn son was presented with the gift of an AK-47. A few weeks after that particular trip to the front, I did a story about a fifteen-year-old commander, Humayun Kadim, whose father, Bolak Kushlaq, died in a Taliban rocket attack while talking to his son over a two-way radio. The Uzbek chief's followers voted unanimously to have Humayun take his father's place as *Amir*, or leader. The boy told me he had three hundred soldiers, six tanks, and a BM-21 Soviet rocket launcher under his command and was studying military tactics and history. He insisted he wasn't afraid to fight. Two of his uncles served as advisers. "We don't let him get too close to battle," one of them told me later. "He's more important as a symbol, and to encourage our people to never give up."

I have no idea what happened to Humayun. But with the Taliban back in power, I don't have much hope for a happy future for him. If he even survived the war.

On the way to Zard Kamar that day, Bartley, Nick, Joao, and I dodged potshots to get to one of the buildings that looked out on the Taliban positions. I interviewed the officer in charge of the assault, a twenty-something with clumps of thick, dark hair fighting for space on his otherwise smooth cheeks. He was nervous, never having been on camera before. But as gunfire popped off in the distance, he described the enemy huddled in buildings barely a hundred feet away. "They are Chechnyan, Chinese [presumably Muslim Uyghurs], and Arabs," he said. "We know for certain al-Qaeda is here."

We watched as figures dressed in all black moved along the alleyways, pausing only to aim and fire in our direction. Bullets thudded against the thick mud walls behind which we huddled. After weeks of covering the struggle, it was obvious to us the war against the Taliban was a day-to-day, grueling, unbelievably dangerous battle of attrition. One that the Northern Alliance had been losing and losing badly for many years, but one that was about to change with the addition of American air power.

This was not an exciting or career-making event in the world of the Afghan people. Theirs was a miserable life of clinging to existence, scraping up enough food and water to provide for their families, working from before sunup to after sundown, and praying to Allah for deliverance.

But for far too many journalists, it was a game, a thrilling way to make a name for oneself. Sometimes, at a horrific cost. A few days after we returned from the first of many trips to the edges of the fighting, we were taping at a location where the Northern Alliance had three ancient tanks emplaced, firing at Taliban soldiers less than a quarter mile away. There were slightly fewer than a dozen journalists present. My notes from that day say that it sounded as though many were speaking Portuguese. It was a rowdy bunch. It was obvious this was the first experience in war for many of them. At one point a female reporter or producer threw a rock and spat at Bartley, saying something about "f-ing Americans"—a terrible insult to our New Zealander cameraman. We could hear some of the reporters urging the tank commander to fire so that they could get different angles of the action, a clear journalistic breach of ethics. Never, ever fake anything, unless you're going to make it clear to viewers that it was a dramatic recreation The commander cheerfully obliged. But we were having none of it, and Bartley put his camera away while the tanks fired.

It was at that point that the order came down for the tanks to attack the Taliban's positions. As they began moving forward, some of the foreign reporters and cameramen climbed onto the armor and hung on, thinking, I can only suppose, that they would get fantastic footage of battle. A few were actually laughing.

There's a thin line between bravery and stupidity. While it's impossible to accurately cover war from a safe location far from the battle lines, those of us who've seen warfare up close have learned that one can push the limits but so far before your luck runs out. No one, least of all clueless civilians, is immortal. It wasn't long before we heard explosions and gunfire in the distance. Within minutes all three tanks returned. Without the journalists on board.

The commander told us that when the Taliban launched a surprise ambush with a superior force, the tanks immediately wheeled about and retreated. But in doing so, all the people riding on top fell off. The tanks, under intense fire, couldn't stop to pick them up.

The Northern Alliance discovered the bodies of the reporters and cameramen days later, strewn across the ground. They had been executed on the spot by the Taliban, one bullet in each head.

The long drive back to Khoja Bahauddin, through the harsh, dusty, wearisome landscape, was done so in silence.

CHAPTER 34

THE OWL AND THE VALUE OF LIFE

October 12, 2001. At the Northern Alliance checkpoint in Afghanistan, half a mile from the front lines of its war against the Taliban, I was busy talking to a sixteen-year-old soldier and didn't notice the owl until it fluttered against the tether that held it to earth. Looking closer I saw that its left wing hung limply, with a splotch of blood near the shoulder joint.

"We shot it," the young man explained, holding up his AK-47 with a discernable measure of pride. He used the Farsi word for owl, *booma*.

It was a beautiful creature, obviously young, with feathered ears that reminded me of the horned owls I admired back home, posing on the branches of the live oaks. The soldier jerked at the cord tied to one of the owl's legs. It stroked at the air with its one good wing and clacked its beak in anger. I bit down the impulse to yank the cord from the boy's hand. But you learn self-control in places where immature people hold deadly weapons. Besides, he would never have understood my anger.

Its feathers were swept with brown and white, soft as eiderdown. They belonged to the winds, not to the dirty ground at the feet of this boy soldier.

I don't know the species, but I'll never forget the bird's eyes. Huge and alert, but tinged with pain. His head swiveled around, and those eyes met mine. They asked me, What new torture do you have to offer?

Gunfire crackled in the distance. I had work to do. We tagged along with some replacement fighters to where a stale-mated battle had waged for weeks and dashed through "snip-er's alley" as the two sides took potshots at each other from the glassless windows of bullet-pocked buildings.

When I returned from the front a few hours later, the owl was still alive.

I offered to buy him from the surprised soldiers, but they handed me the cord and said, basically, "Help yourself."

"But take care," they added. "He can rip you open." When his talons clamped around my wrist moments later, he proved them right.

For some reason I felt the need to explain this action to the soldiers. I asked our translator to tell them I wanted to try to save him. He looked at me incredulously. "Go on, tell them," I urged him. With a shrug, he repeated what I asked him to say. They blinked at him, then at me, and then erupted in laughter. Such was the response all the way back to our camp. I rode in the back of the pickup truck, with the owl held in my lap, wrapped in a cloth, and whenever we answered their curious looks, they laughed.

"But we shoot them," they would say. "We shoot the boomas. Why would you want to save it?"

"Because all life is precious," I would respond. "Doesn't the Quran say so?"

And they would shrug, say yes, and laugh again.

Of course, it's completely understandable that if you've killed other people and seen your friends killed, and maybe your brother, or father, then the entire perception of life becomes somewhat nebulous.

One of the Afghanis took the time to explain why they kill owls. The soldiers prefer to shoot game birds, pheasants and quail, while they roost on the ground. It's easier that way. And it has nothing to do with sport: The birds are good food.

But the owls have a different hunting technique. They fly overhead and drop stones where the birds are hiding, causing them to fly up. The owls, perhaps a more sporting species than humans, will only take their prey on the wing, not on the ground. Unfortunately, that spoils the soldier's chance at dinner. So they shoot the boomas.

To these men, the equation is simple. The owls make it harder to get dinner; therefore, the owls are a nuisance. It's not a matter of morality. It's a matter of food.

On the long ride back to our news media compound at Khoja Bahauddin, I made a decision: If the owl I held in my lap lived through the night, I would try to save it. But if it was suffering, I'd put it out of its misery.

At 4:00 a.m. that morning, I heard a noise in the corner of my little cramped tent where I'd stowed the bird in a cardboard box, and when I peered in, I saw him looking around, alert and curious, even a little bit feisty. That made the decision for me.

The next day I raided the compound's medical supplies and spent three hours, a veterinary amateur, cleaning the wound with rubbing alcohol and splinting the broken wing bone with two tongue depressors. I didn't know if it would ever fly again, but it obviously wanted to live. Maybe it would become a camp mascot, I thought. Maybe I'd make it a gift to the local government.

For a moment I actually allowed myself to think he was going to pull through. To my surprise, the owl took a drink of water when offered and ate a bite of raw cow liver. I thought that was a wonderfully good sign.

So when I returned from working on a story later that night and found him lying limp in the bottom of the box, I could only hope that I hadn't prolonged its suffering.

With all the death and suffering the Afghan people had and were enduring, the life of an owl was inconsequential. I knew that. But it also occurred to me that the owl was a symbol of the long way Afghanistan, and perhaps humanity itself, has to go before the simple pleasure of watching a magnificent bird riding the air is perceived not as a threat but as a gift.

CHAPTER 35

DUST TO DUST

Through the binoculars, ominous figures in dark robes could be seen moving about the mountain ridges to the west. This was the Taliban's front line near the city of Kunduz, dotted with mortar emplacements and riven with trenches carved into the beige, barren ground. Intermingled were soldiers in fatigues, but it was the mysterious black-clad men who sent a chill up the spine.

Osama bin Laden's al-Qaeda organization had soldiers and training camps scattered throughout Afghanistan, even in the north. General Mohammed Ayun, the Northern Alliance commander in charge of this region along the Kowkcheh River, said he had captured Taliban fighters who were Arabic-speaking, Chechen (from the region of Russia undergoing its own tortured civil war), or even Chinese, which the general said meant they were al-Qaeda mercenaries.

One thing was for sure: the figures in black were clearly not from around here. Here was a place it had taken us six hours of grueling travel over mountain and desert and riverbed to reach, slammed back and forth in a four-wheel-drive Toyota pickup that had been liberated from al-Qaeda by Alliance troops. It was two weeks after my arrival in Afghanistan and my fourth trip to one of the myriad front lines.

The Northern Alliance held the high ground overlooking Kunduz. They were pushed into these dusky peaks by a Taliban offensive the year before that robbed the Alliance of the city and a supply road to armies in the north near the oft-contested key city of Mazar-e Sharif. It was a devastating loss, but General Ayun ordered the retreat when he saw the Taliban shelling Kunduz itself, causing massive civilian casualties. Rather than watch the destruction of innocent lives and a beautiful city, he pulled his men back into these mountain parapets and began the long chess game of tank and mortar fire.

Along the ridges, the Alliance had set up a series of bunkers and gun emplacements. There were Soviet-era T-55 tanks buried up to their turrets for added protection, which, as of a few weeks previously, was evidently no longer that necessary. A lucky or amazingly accurate shot from an Alliance tank took out the Taliban's only artillery gun capable of reaching the mountaintops, so the Alliance fighters rained shells on their enemy's positions at their leisure. They did so infrequently, though, because they were saving their ammunition for the day, soon to come, they said, when the American air strikes softened up the Taliban sufficiently and the time came to roll down from the heights and retake Kunduz. That was the day they were all praying for.

Late one night, we shivered in the cold as we watched the lights of Taliban vehicles moving around in the valley below and the occasional rooster tail of antiaircraft tracers lift into the skies, reaching out for high-altitude American warplanes, either real or imagined. Overhead, though, the only thing visible to us was the stunning light show from a zillion stars on this moonless night, the Milky Way stretched out like salt cast onto a deep-blue tablecloth. I caught myself wanting to tell Katie about this sight; she, who would point out Orion's Belt or Cassiopeia and then stare upward far longer than I would—out of appreciation or simply just daydreaming. She seemed as far away now as those stars.

A soldier's face materialized out of the dark next to me, lit up by a match that flared and was quickly extinguished, giving way to the glow of a cigarette cherry. Almost all the soldiers smoke here, and after a few weeks of enduring the relentless windstorms that sent talc-like dust into our tents and mouths and lungs, compared to just breathing the air, smoking began to seem like a benign habit. The dust had become a fifth element of existence for us in northern Afghanistan, pervasive and invasive and relentless. I took to bathing once a week, not just for lack of water, but since I was immediately coated with a fine patina of beige as soon as I toweled off, I simply began to wonder: what was the point?

The soldier, whom I dubbed "Canada" for the one, albeit incongruous, word he knew of English, offered me a drag, and I declined. The night was cemetery quiet. We could see no jets, nor could we hear any. The Americans had struck here the two preceding evenings, and we were hoping to witness another air strike this night. A handful of Alliance soldiers hung around with us, even though most of their comrades were cozy and warm in their bunkers, one of which was equipped with a black-and- white television set powered by a bootleg generator. The movie tonight was *Broadcast News*, dubbed in Pashto, I think. I thought back on the best lines from that film— William Hurt: "What do you do when your life exceeds your dreams?" Albert Brooks: "Keep it to yourself."

One of the sentries, also named Mohammed Ayun—no relation to the general—knelt down next to us and put his hands together at the wrists in the sign of bondage. "Taliban," he said. It turns out he'd been a prisoner of war for a year and still had his International Committee of the Red Cross prisoner-exchange voucher. He kept it in a small leather wallet hanging from a thong around his neck, like some kind of talisman. Or, maybe, a get-out-of-jail-free card.

It was when he lifted his shirt and showed me a still-suppurating bullet wound in his stomach that I began to understand the determination these men have to rid their country of the Taliban. Ayun had been wounded three times, held captive for over a year, only fed one piece of bread in the morning, and here he stood, as close to the enemy as a John Elway touchdown pass. "I don't have a choice," he said. "They come here, they invade our country, they ruin our lives. We have to fight."

Given Afghanistan's history of dealing with uninvited visitors, from Genghis Khan to the British to the Soviets, I'd say the odds favor the Afghanis. The invaders always leave with fewer men than they came with. And the Taliban, being largely from Pakistan or Arabic countries, are seen as a foreign presence. It is, however, part of the complexity of this land that the Alliance is largely composed of ethnic groups from other areas, too, Tajiks and Uzbeks and Shiites, but they consider themselves to be Afghani as well.

At a little after 1:00 a.m., the Taliban sent a stream of antiaircraft fire skyward over Kunduz, but no bombs rained down on the front lines. Instead, we saw three enormous flashes of light far to the north that could only have been caused by huge explosions. We found out later the only thing in that area that could've been a target was a suspected al-Qaeda training camp. The fist of American retribution was reaching out for those it held responsible for the loss and sorrow and inhumanity of the September 11 attacks, and throughout this parched, impossibly rugged country, terrorists were beginning to learn what real terror was.

Weeks later, during a brief respite from my assignment covering the war for ABC News, which had decided, after all, to renew my contract, I walked down to the block where the World Trade Center once stood and watched the cranes lift huge, perversely twisted sections of seven-foot-wide steel girders. In the short time I had back home, Katie and I were slowly trying to reconnect, trying to reach that place of wordless trust and comfort that had existed before the sound of the low-flying jet ripped a hole in our lives and sucked us into this alternate universe that still seemed foreign and unreal. I couldn't get the map of our future folded back the way it goes, no matter how I wrestled with it, and all the plans we'd made didn't quite seem to fit together anymore.

A piece of paper blew past, drawing my eye downward, and I noticed I was still wearing the Jean Baptiste Rautureau boots I'd picked up in Soho years ago, the same sturdy pair that had accompanied me to Kosovo and Croatia, to Columbine and Oklahoma City. These boots had supported me during some of my toughest assignments, the leather molding itself to my feet, shielding me against rock and thorn and fatigue, and I dread the day they finally wear out. I take better care of those boots than I do my own teeth; two retreads, and there's always time at the airport for a quick stop at the shoeshine stand no matter how tight the airline connection.

But this afternoon I saw they were not their normally polished black gloss; rather, they were a drab, filthy greyish brown. And I realized, because of the hurried forty-eight hours of travel that had brought me back from Afghanistan without a stop along the way, that they still carried on them the dust of Khoja Bahauddin, the dregs of frontline trenches from a fight against shadowy foes, the desiccated topsoil of a country wracked by years of drought and despair. I lifted my foot and stomped down on the concrete at the corner of Broadway and Liberty Plaza.

A small cloud rose from the top of the boot, and a small cloud rose from under its sole, the pervasive residue from September 11 that still and may forever coat the buildings and streets of lower Manhattan. The two puffs floated together, dust to dust, before dissipating on the breeze.

I have learned that the world is an immensely large place connected by the smallest of things. I have learned that people have the capacity for hate and violence that exceed all reason, and for generosity and bravery that exceed all logic. I have learned that knowledge does not equal understanding.

And I have learned that our lives spin in no certain direction at a terrifying speed. It's a far better journey if you have a tight grip on someone else.

CHAPTER 36

THE DAILY SHOW

"Welcome back to the show! My guest tonight is an ABC News correspondent who has just returned from northern Afghanistan. He reports for *Good Morning America*, *World News Tonight*, and *20/20*...please welcome Don Dahler. Don!"

That's how Jon Stewart introduced me in late October 2001, just a day after I'd landed back in New York City. I hadn't even had time to get a much-needed haircut, so I walked out onto *The Daily Show* stage looking like an aging member of a boy band.

Jon was still relatively new to the program, having taken over for the insufferable Craig Kilborn not quite two years earlier, and his producers were determined to have their extremely smart and funny new host tackle more serious subjects, not just snarky takes on the latest celebrity hijinks.

"Thank you for coming by the program..."

"My pleasure."

"Where were you in Afghanistan? You were just there."

"Just there. The northern area near a town called Khoja Bahauddin."

"Which, I hear, is lovely this time of year," he joked. I had to bite back a chuckle.

"Yes, it is."

"What kind of a town is that? Ten thousand people? Twenty thousand people?"

"Well, I think it's about a hundred thousand people and two hundred thousand goats." So much for my cultural sensitivity. But we were going for laughs as well as information.

I was dressed casually, in a loose crewneck sweater under a black suede jacket and black jeans. Jon, on the other hand, was wearing a nice suit and tie. Back then he had dark hair, which is now a glorious silver.

"Are you staying in a hotel there with other reporters?" Again, I could barely stifle a laugh. Noting my reaction, Jon said, "Am I not getting this at all?"

"You're not getting this. It's a very undeveloped part of the country..."

"Yeah," he replied sarcastically, "the rest of it's very cosmopolitan."

"We lived in tents inside a mud-walled compound. And right outside my tent was the brick-making factory, which consisted of a pit where a man stomped on cow dung, straw, and mud to make these bricks"—Jon put his hand over his face as the audience chuckled—"so the odor in the morning was worth getting out of bed for."

"Can I tell you," Jon said, "that is exactly like my stoop here in the city."

Between covering the attacks on the World Trade Center live and being one of the first American journalists inside Afghanistan before the US launched its war against the Taliban, I had gotten quite a bit of attention from media outlets. Oprah Winfrey even featured me in her enormously popular show. Stewart's program was one of my favorites, though, and I was delighted to get the request to be on it.

The tricky part, of course, was being relaxed and funny without being inappropriate. Jon was well informed and inquisitive, and we talked about Afghanistan's history with invaders, including the Soviets, and the rugged countryside.

Stepping out of my objectivity for a moment, I described the Taliban as an evil regime that was unbelievably cruel to its own people. (It still is.)

The *Daily Show* host pressed, "You see no moral uncertainty within this war? These guys have got to go?"

"From everything I could gather from the Afghanis I talked to, the Taliban is kind of a combination between *Lord of the Flies* and Darth Vader. They are the most warped individuals..."

"Really?" Jon interrupted. "In what sense?"

"For news people, we compiled a list to keep track of who the Taliban were." I explained that at the top of the list was Mullah Omar, the Taliban's leader, who never actually went to religious school. The commerce minister, who, in addition to having no formal education, was missing an eye. "They have a couple designations so that you can recognize these individuals, missing an eye, missing an arm, missing a foot, missing half their frontal lobe..." Jon liked that one.

We talked about the warlords whose avarice created the climate for the rise of the Taliban and extremist elements, and whether the recent US air campaign was popular with the Afghan people. He then asked what kind of information they were getting about the American operation: "I know we drop pamphlets on them that say, uh, 'Yankees good!' You know, 'Love chocolate!'" Big laugh from the audience.

"There are two forms of mass communication in the country," I explained. "There used to be three, but the Taliban banned television. Except for themselves."

"They should really get cable," Jon interjected.

"Yeah, there are a couple good shows on cable we all like," I replied. "One of [the forms of information] is: BBC has this multilanguage radio broadcasts, and you see these guys walking around with these little Walkman radios listening, and the other form of mass communication is the town crier, who wanders around and literally will shout out the news for anyone to hear. Now usually it's whose donkey died and why, that kind of thing. But they also will spread, you know, 'the Americans are dropping food...look up!'"

"There's a guy that's literally walking around town [yelling things]?"

"Yeah."

"Again, we have that here!" Another big laugh.

"Yeah, but their guy makes sense."

"Oh, so he's not just walking around saying, 'Furniture tastes crispy!'"

We closed out the segment with a smart question from Jon about Ramadan, and whether the US should curtail its bombing runs out of sensitivity to the Muslim holiday. Fortunately, I knew the history of conflict in the Muslim world and how wars were often continued despite the holy days.

I was truly sorry when my eight minutes were up, and we said goodbye. Jon Stewart showed that humor and intelligent, important conversations can coexist.

There were, however, no bookers clamoring for me to join the comedy club circuit. After about a two-week break, I was back in Afghanistan. Just in time for winter and a violent end to the Taliban's rule.

CHAPTER 37

TIME TO GO

We could see the B-52s overhead, leaving contrails behind them in the frigid high-altitude air as they dropped a series of five-hundred-pound bombs on the Taliban fighters in the trees and houses of the valley below. The bombs, as they fell, weren't visible to the human eye, but the explosions were teeth rattling.

The Northern Alliance commander standing on the mountaintop next to me grew concerned. "The bombs," he told my translator. "They're getting too close to my soldiers!"

Sure enough, I felt myself lifted three feet off the ground by the next blast, which couldn't have been more than a half mile away. Without a doubt, dozens—if not hundreds—of Northern Alliance soldiers stationed at the mountain's base had just been blown to pieces. Drew Millhon, the ABC producer working with me, placed a sat phone call to New York, asking if there was anyone who could kindly suggest to the Pentagon that their bombs were off target.

As the munitions continued to fall, I did a videophone report from the mountaintop, and then Drew, Franzi, Alex, and I climbed into our two four-wheel-drive vehicles and started back to the nearby town of Taloqan, where we were based. Fifteen minutes into the drive, a streak of high-caliber tracer rounds passed directly in front of our truck's windscreen.

No one was hit, but we sped up as fast as the trucks could go. A bad wheel bearing on our Toyota made it feel as though we were being shaken to death inside a washing machine.

As the noose was tightening around the Taliban's necks, Afghanistan was becoming progressively more dangerous for us, not less.

We'd been on our way from Khoja Bahauddin to Kabul when the fighting around the city of Kunduz blocked our way, so we ended up hanging around a week or so to cover the siege of what was the last stronghold of the Taliban in the north.

After a ten-hour trek past dun-colored mountains, donkey caravans loaded with lumber and food, and rusty corpses of Soviet-era tanks and crossing countless bridgeless rivers, we pulled into Taloqan after dark on November 15. Our translator, Dr. Habib Rustaque, a twenty-nine-year-old surgeon specializing in war injuries, found a suitable compound right next to the Foreign Ministry's new base of operations to house us and our drivers, twelve people in all. But as we were setting up camp, a military truck pulled into the courtyard, and a Northern Alliance officer announced a General Mujibullah was arriving soon and would commandeer the house for himself.

Habib found a new place for us in short order, not far away; the house of a judge who'd fled the country. His houseboy, who looked to be about eighty, negotiated the rent—$500 for the week. He'd draw an extra ten dollars a day to keep things clean. Drew and Habib went out to hire some guards while the rest of us, including our editor, Larry Waxman, started organizing what was to be our headquarters for the foreseeable future.

The sounds of distant explosions and gunfire never seemed to stop, day and night. When we weren't at the front lines, Franzi, Habib, and I would venture into Taloqan's outdoor market to buy food. We'd finished the last of our MREs and granola bars a few days earlier. There were no real restaurants or processed dinners in the grocery stores—in fact, there were no grocery stores period, just stalls of fresh vegetables, fruit, live chickens, and slabs of beef.

The Afghanis in town seemed friendly and curious. Habib said many of them expressed gratitude that the Americans were finally involved in ridding their country of the invaders, meaning the Taliban. The men often waved to us and smiled; the women, of course, pulled their veils across their faces and looked away. Children ran alongside, chattering away and high-fiving the foreigners.

We took turns making dinner. Franzi and Alex were great at crepes. I leaned more toward spaghetti or soup. I found this scribbled down on one of the pages of my journal:

> Recipe for Taloqan Soup
> Peel & slice a dozen large onions
> Let cook down in large pot
> to caramelized state
> Add 1 litre water
> ½ doz peeled & cut carrots
> ½ doz peeled chunk potatoes
> Paprika, salt, tobacco
> ½ bunch chopped cilantro
> 2 squares chicken bullion
> Let simmer. Go to live shots.
> Return. Enjoy.

When we got back from an assignment at a nearby refugee center on the nineteenth, we heard from one of the guys who worked for an international satellite transmission company that a caravan of journalists, who were traveling from Jalalabad to Kabul, were ambushed by either bandits or the Taliban. They were taken from their vehicles at gunpoint, marched up a hill, and shot to death.

We had a team meeting that night and decided we would stay until Kunduz fell, then head home. We'd pushed our luck far enough.

The Northern Alliance general in charge of the area, Mohammed Daud Daud, gave the Taliban an ultimatum: surrender within two days or face annihilation. The high-altitude bombing stopped during the ceasefire, but as we traveled around the region, the sound of machine-gun fire was still constant. Trucks and cars loaded with hundreds of Alliance soldiers were streaming into the area. But even so, we all sensed something had changed. General Daud had promised the Taliban that if they surrendered, they would be welcomed back into society without penalty, so dozens of black-clad soldiers were making their way out of Kunduz and back to Taloqan. For some inconceivable reason, the Alliance did not insist they give up their weapons. Daud, incidentally, was rewarded for his generosity by being assassinated by the Taliban in 2011.

Our trips to the market were becoming steadily more tense, with dark looks from the locals. At one point, a small boy punched me hard in the arm and said what I can only assume was a curse. Rather than reprimanding him, the adults around him laughed.

On November 22, the word come down that the Taliban had formally surrendered Kunduz, but the sound of distant tank fire indicated that not everyone was done fighting. We later confirmed that was a false report. Quite a few Taliban had, indeed, crossed the lines and surrendered, but pockets were still holding on.

That evening Franzi tried her best to make a Thanksgiving-like feast for the Americans on our team: pasta with tomato sauce piled up in the shape of a turkey and local pastries. Alex, unfortunately, missed the celebration, having been bedridden from inhaling toxic gas that leaked from a Russian propane heater. We were all very worried about him. It takes a lot to knock down a tough guy his size. Later that night we were all awakened by an enormous blast that billowed in the plastic sheets that covered the house's windows. A contact with the State Department told me the US Air Force dropped a fifteen-thousand-pound "daisy cutter" bomb on a nearby al-Qaeda training camp.

As the siege continued, we made air on every ABC newscast, from the early morning show to *Nightline*. It was thrilling and important, but exhausting. Finally, we all got a day off on Saturday the twenty-fourth. Most of the team slept while I sat up writing and listening to music on my portable CD player—Marvin Gaye, Roy Orbison, and Bob Dylan.

The next day, Kunduz finally fell. We watched from the mountaintop as Taliban soldiers walked out of the shattered city to be greeted by the cheers and hugs from their former enemies, the Northern Alliance. The only word I could think of to describe our reaction was *gobsmacked*. It was time to go. That night we began making plans to pack up and depart as soon as possible after fulfilling our assignments for the various newscasts. Predictably there was a high degree of interest in our coverage, so we were booked for multiple live or taped reports over the next few days.

That Monday I stayed up late, writing and voicing a piece for *World News Tonight* with Larry, our editor. At some point that evening, we heard the sound of gunfire, closer than usual. We passed it off as just more Taliban holdouts getting their comeuppance. We could not have been more wrong.

At about 1:30 a.m., after I recorded my voice for the *WNT* story, Larry and Drew drove a few blocks to the nearby European Broadcast Union satellite feed point to send it back to New York. I slipped into my sleeping bag and fell into a deep slumber.

I'm not sure how long I was asleep, but I awoke to Franzi standing over me with a lantern. She said a journalist had been murdered a few houses away. Drew and Larry were staying put at the EBU site until morning. After much effort we got ahold of Drew on a sat phone, and, despite a lousy connection and Drew's understandably shaken nerves, I pieced together what happened. It wasn't until I got back to the US that I found out the victim's name.

Three gunmen wearing black clothes and turbans, the uniform of the Taliban, broke into a house a few hundred feet from where we were staying. They first demanded money from two newspaper reporters, threatening to kill them if they didn't cooperate. The journalists handed over cash, cameras, and cell phones. The gunmen then fired several times through the door of the room where Swedish cameraman Ulf Strömberg was staying when he refused to let them in. A bullet struck the forty-two-year-old in the chest. At that point, the assailants fled.

Strömberg collapsed into the arms of one of his coworkers and said, "I'm shot. I'm dying." As they lay him on the floor, he told them, "My legs are cold." Not even an hour earlier he'd spoken to his wife and three children over a sat phone.

The Swedish reporters put him into their vehicle and drove to the EBU location to see if anyone could help them find a hospital. That's where Drew and Larry found out about the attack. It was decided it was simply too dangerous for the reporters to travel anywhere else at night, so Drew sent Mustaba, one of our local drivers, with the injured man in one of our Toyotas to the hospital. On the way there another group of four masked armed men stopped the vehicle and searched it before ultimately letting them continue.

Our translator, Habib, happened to be at the hospital when they arrived. Even with his surgical trauma training, there was nothing he could do for Strömberg. He was already dead from a severed aorta. On the way back to the EBU truck, Habib and Mustaba were confronted yet again by a group of men waving AK-47s, but the two were waved through after another search. They arrived at our house, ashen-faced and scared.

We set about breaking down the editing equipment and packing up the trucks that night. At dawn, Drew and I went back to the satellite feed truck to do a live debrief about the situation in the area for *Nightline*. I mentioned the presence of Taliban in the area and the murder. It would be our last broadcast from Afghanistan.

One of the local Alliance commanders we'd come to know offered to accompany us back to the border, along with four of his soldiers—for a price, of course. With the Northern Alliance forces pushing southward toward Kabul, the road to Khoja and ultimately to Tajikistan was becoming increasingly more dangerous. Taliban and bandits were everywhere. Alex, thankfully, was back to his healthy self. Having served in the Austrian military, and out of concern for Franzi, he felt strongly we should also carry weapons. So did I. The Alliance lent us some AK-47s. Unlike the rules of embedding with the US military, we had signed no document promising to be noncombatants. We were not going to become yet more helpless victims without a fight.

As soon as the other journalists in town found out we were leaving, they clamored to join our convoy, delaying our departure by a few hours. But eventually we started the long, dusty, difficult trek back to the Panj River. Thankfully we encountered no trouble along the way.

A few days later, during my three-hour layover in Moscow, I got a message from Chuck Lustig, the head of ABC's foreign desk. "Take a long break. You've done enough. Go home." He then, perhaps prophetically, added, "Things are heating up in Iraq."

CHAPTER 38

DID YOU HEAR THE ONE ABOUT LEO DICAPRIO?

Our fire escape overlooked the Hudson River and the West Side Highway, easily accessed by opening one of the large arched floor-to-ceiling windows. On it, a man sat, smoking a cigarette and thinking. Inside the apartment, his stunningly beautiful girlfriend danced around the loft with our one-year-old daughter in her arms, laughing and cooing. Katie and I shared a silent look of amazement between us that said, Can you believe this?

We had bought the Tribeca apartment three years earlier, shortly after we were married, and sank every spare dime we had into renovations. The brick warehouse building, which had stood silent witness when Abraham Lincoln's funeral procession left the Hudson River Railroad station for its trip through Manhattan in 1865, was a classic marvel of exposed brick, floor-to-ceiling arched windows, and wooden beams. Trolley tracks were still visible on the floors. That particular apartment was originally a completely open space with views on the north, south, and west sides. The only walls enclosed the small bathroom. We upgraded the bathroom, put in a new kitchen and gas fireplace, and partitioned off a small master bedroom and even smaller kid's room.

It was a fluke we had it at all. Like many New Yorkers, we would spend weekends wandering from open house to open house just to see how the 1 percent lived, and this place, at the corner of Canal Street and the West Side Highway, was one such jewel—priced, at first inspection, way above our means. But about a year after we first toured the sixth-floor condo, I was walking up West Broadway and noticed a man pasting a new photo in the window of his quirky real estate office. I immediately recognized it as the Tribeca loft. I watched as he taped the words "Drastically Reduced" next to the photo. When I went inside, the realtor informed me, to my shock, the price was now at the exact upper limit of our budget.

Katie answered her phone on the first ring. "Remember that apartment by the river?" I said. "It's up for sale again with a reduced price."

"How reduced?" she asked. I told her. "Put an offer on it!" I did. Within days, we were under contract.

Turns out that the loft had served as a pied-à-terre for a local restaurateur, who, rumor had it, used it strictly for trysts with his lovely young waitresses and hostesses. One of his establishments ran into financial trouble, and he was forced to raise cash, thus the fire sale of the Tribeca loft. When I was bashing apart the built-in king-sized bed he'd put in one corner of the living space, I found dozens of nude photos of various women that had fallen under the mattress and a few love notes from his wife in Italy, who, if I understood the language correctly, missed him dearly.

It was a magical place we could never have imagined owning. Every afternoon the sun set directly across the Hudson, painting the inside of the apartment golden orange. We were within walking distance of some of the best restaurants in town, and my commute to the ABC studios was a quick subway ride uptown. Eventually Katie, who, while pregnant, endured living in a plastic dust-invaded bubble as the renovations dragged on, gave birth to our daughter, and we spent the next few years raising her as a true New York baby. I hung a small bear-shaped swing from one of the beams in which she would spend hours giggling and kicking with joy, and she learned to walk along the Hudson River Park and in the Central Park Zoo. On weekends people would constantly greet us with smiles and waves, to our surprise, until I noticed a tiny hand waving from the side of the BabyBjörn in which I was carrying Callie on my chest. Everyone was a friend to our little girl.

But when Katie got pregnant with our second child, Jack, we determined the apartment was too small for the four of us. There was simply no elegant way to divide it up further into a three bedroom. So we decided to list it for sale. The timing couldn't have been better—Manhattan was in the middle of a real estate boom.

If memory serves, it was only a day or two before we got a call from our listing agent that "a famous actor would like to see the apartment." He couldn't tell me who it was. "He's very private," he explained. The actor and his girlfriend wanted a "cool place in Tribeca" to call home whenever they came to the East Coast.

When the appointed day came, I opened the door and looked into the strikingly handsome eyes of Jack Dawson, whom I'd last seen clinging to the side of a floating door before sliding into the icy waters of the northern Atlantic. Yes, it was Leonardo DiCaprio in the flesh. And, standing slightly behind him, and a few inches taller, was the future ex–Mrs. Tom Brady: Gisele Bündchen.

They honestly could not have been nicer and more down-to-earth. The couple and their realtor wandered around our home, commenting on the wonderful raw brick and rough-hewn beams. At some point Gisele spotted Callie in her bouncy chair and lost all interest in the loft. She spent the rest of the time carrying our daughter around, chatting with her, and engaging her in playtime. Leo excused himself for a smoke and climbed through one of the large, hinged windows to sit on the fire escape and watch the traffic flow by.

One or both of them came back to see the apartment a total of six times over the next two weeks. Sometimes they would sit on our big, plush couch and just chat, with Callie always snuggled into Gisele's lap.

We were getting a lot of interest from other buyers, so the realtor gently suggested they make a move or risk losing it. For one last visit Leo asked to bring his 80-year-old grandmother up for her blessing. It just so happened that was the day of a major power outage all over Manhattan, but the two DiCaprios made their way up six flights of stairs to have another look. He put a full-price offer on it later that day.

The next morning the realtor called and informed us there was a competing bid from a financial industries type. He tried to reach Leo, but the actor was away in a remote location on a film shoot, and his agent didn't have the authority to up their offer. In the end we had to take the higher bid, and DiCaprio bought a place further up the street in a fantastic modern architectural marvel that had the same views but perhaps not as much character as our funky little loft.

It was with mixed feelings that we packed everything up and moved away from Tribeca. We made enough from the sale to buy an old house with a big yard in New Jersey, where we eventually welcomed our son into the family. Who, by the way, is still jealous that his sister had been danced around the room in the arms of a supermodel.

CHAPTER 39

NONE FLEW OVER THE CUCKOO'S NEST

It came in the form of an email: a polite, lengthy note from a self-described documentarian in northern Europe who claimed to have irrefutable evidence that the 9/11 attacks didn't really happen the way the public had been led to believe. He included a link to his latest film, which was to air on public access TV within a few months, and, as I was the first network correspondent who reported live from the scene at Ground Zero, he was seeking my response to his theories.

I'm not going to mention his name or the network on which his film aired because I don't want to give either of them any further advertisement. But let's just say that he's passionately, deliberately, indefatigably ignorant.

Normally I never respond to these kinds of messages. They are so damn tiresome. Most are from people who seized on my description of the jet as it flew over lower Manhattan as "sounding like a missile." Or when I told Peter Jennings the World Trade Center building collapsed "like when you see an old building demolished by explosives." Countless conspiracy theorists have taken those two comments out of context and run with them. "Reporter Didn't See Airplane" is the typical headline that they use in a quixotic effort to prove 9/11 was an inside job conducted by the US government, ignoring the fact that the second plane entered the building opposite of where I was standing, so I couldn't possibly have seen it. They talk of "thermite explosives," which, in their fever dreams, is what actually brought down the twin towers; claim that jet fuel couldn't possibly burn at a high enough temperature to melt steel girders (wrong); and expound at length about "the missing plane" they insist didn't really hit the Pentagon. "Look how low the jet would've had to fly to enter the building at that angle!" one writes, forgetting, I guess, that airplanes all fly that low when they're doing a little thing called "landing."

It's astounding how many pretzel shapes people will twist their logic into just to disprove the easily provable. Kennedy was killed by multiple shooters, they declare. Hilary Clinton is a cannibalistic pedophile who frequents pizza parlors. The moon landing took place in a Hollywood sound stage. Contrails are a government plot to give us all cancer or spontaneous abortions. The 2020 election was tainted by hundreds of thousands of illegal votes. Yet the actual evidence of their rabid imaginations is never, ever, ever brought forth. Enthusiastic theories, yes. Evidence, no.

The filmmaker (and I use that term hesitantly) seemed sincere in his request for an objective opinion from me, so I decided to give his documentary a serious examination.

He led with the conclusion that video experts created everything that happened on September 11, 2001, on computers. Sitting in his apartment almost four thousand miles away, he had diligently recorded hours of news media coverage from that day and set about analyzing it all frame by frame. I won't repeat every ridiculous allegation, but his general thesis was based on glitches and video anomalies he claimed showed digital manipulation.

After watching his entire presentation, I responded with a point-by-point refutation—the ultimate conclusion being that when you record video off the internet that has likely already been copied and, thus, degraded multiple times, there's going to be a fraying of the pixels. It's just natural. The "shimmering frames of the plane going into the building" doesn't indicate a digital overlay; it indicates that the images he was using were third or fourth generation.

But more than that, my main point was how he completely ignored the tens of thousands, perhaps hundreds of thousands, of witnesses on the ground in New York and DC who saw the plane crashes, and subsequent building collapses, with their own eyes. This wasn't a controlled incident that could easily be explained as manufactured in a government office—we all saw it happen in real time.

He never bothered to respond to my critique and, I assume, didn't include any of it in his film when it aired. And he's by no means alone.

Conspiracy theorists really, really hate being proven wrong. That's why they all claim the fake media is part of the cover up. One wacko compiled a timeline of various reports, side by side, which he alleged showed I was reporting for ABC and Fox under two fake identities to push a false narrative, because the other reporter and I were never on the air at the same time. Another insisted I was a known CIA officer putting a spin on the event, and that I jumped in to redirect Peter Jennings's musings about whether the buildings could have come down from explosives set off at their base. Yes, I did, indeed, correct Peter when he pondered that, because it was obvious from my perspective that the collapses both happened when the top parts of the buildings lost their structural integrity due to the incredibly hot flames and toppled.

I'm sure there are quite a few doctorates awarded to those who have studied such mass delusions. Some people simply mistrust the official record and are desperate to find an alternative meaning. I get that, but it has to make *sense*. There are millions of folks walking around alive today because they got childhood vaccinations who nevertheless believe the COVID vaccines are deadly, despite every bit of medical evidence to the contrary.

A terrifying number of people still actually believe the 2012 Sandy Hook massacre of twenty-seven children and teachers was a "false flag" attempt by the government to take away guns. And simply because I covered that horrible tragedy, I was targeted as part of the disinformation campaign. That I reported on numerous such events over the decades only underlined my reputation among the cultists as a crisis actor, along with the—in their minds—make-believe grieving parents and nonexistent young lives snuffed out so horribly.

I don't know what the answer to this phenomenon is. The uninformed opinion distribution powers of the internet and social media are only getting stronger and more disturbingly radical and unhinged. QAnon is a perfect example of this. If a large percentage of our population refuses to believe certifiable, provable truths, then what is the basis of any meaningful understanding?

There's a philosophical principle known as Occam's razor, which is sometimes misinterpreted as "the simplest explanation is usually the best one." Actually, it really means that the most effective explanations are those with the fewest parts. Most of what happens in the world is not overly complex. Bad people do bad things. Good people suffer from them.

And internet trolls feed on, exploit, and profit from the misery of so many innocent people. I yearn for the days when people were held accountable for their hateful comments, dangerous conspiracies, and dishonesty.

CHAPTER 40

FRIENDS OR FOES?

We huddled down in the narrow skiff, painfully aware of the sound the little motor was making as we peered across the Euphrates River, trying earnestly to spot some signal flashlights on the other side. The sun was climbing up the eastern horizon but had not yet broken through. In those predawn moments, producer James Franklin Blue, videographer extraordinaire Alex Bruckner, Alex's sound person and future wife Franziska "Franzi" Neidhart, a handful of Kurdish rebels, and I were surreptitiously making our way from Syria into northern Iraq. The furtive river crossing was the culmination of months of coded communications and an illegal nighttime dash across the length of Syria in a darkened sedan, without visas, without journalistic credentials, without any hope of diplomatic cover in the unfortunate event we were detained by the Syrian special police. It was an enormously risky operation. One I am, to this day, enormously proud of.

Our mission was to reach the Kurds of northern Iraq to find out if they would fight with, or against, the US in the inevitable war against Saddam Hussein's regime. There was no other way to get there. Iraq was in lockdown in anticipation of the coming invasion. There was a no-fly zone over its northern regions. No journalists from the West had been in meaningful contact with the Kurdish rebel groups for over a decade. And we were not at all sure if we'd receive a welcome committee on the far shore or a barrage of gunfire. Leroy Sievers and Tom Bettag, the legendary co–executive producers of Ted Koppel's *Nightline*, had approved the project. To this day I'm not positive they knew, or wanted to know, the risks we took.

Back then, ABC News's *Nightline* was every bit the journalistic match of CBS's *60 Minutes*, in terms of content, investigative reporting, and story breaking. The best journalism I ever did was for that program. When Larry died of a brain tumor and Tom and Ted were forced out, the DC-based unit was gutted and defanged. But they were, in those days, the "SEAL Team" of broadcast journalism. Fearless, inventive, original, and absolutely committed to journalistic integrity.

As we neared the Iraqi side of the river, we spotted a few flashes of light. The boat's skipper throttled back, and we sloughed into the muddy bank. Whispered sentences were offered between a man at the front of our little boat and the unseen fellows on the shore.

"It's good," our translator reported, with obvious relief. "They're our guys."

For the next several weeks, we lived and worked in the unofficially recognized nation of Kurdistan. Two *Nightline* programs resulted from our efforts. And it was eye opening to the American public. When Ted Koppel introduced our first dispatch, he said, with obvious surprise, "The extraordinary thing is that the Kurds do seem willing to make common cause with the United States again."

Quite some time later, I traveled through Iraq with the 101st Airborne. I saw firsthand the squalor, the lack of infrastructure, that contrasted with the palaces and opulence of Saddam's supporters. Kurdistan, when our little crew ventured into its towns and villages, stood in shocking relief.

First, the highways were excellent—paved and well marked. The towns had fully stocked grocery stores, restaurants, ice cream parlors, beauty salons, and even amusement parks. People seemed happy and healthy. Women not only eschewed the Islam-mandated burkas and veils; they held public office and ran businesses. Girls sat next to boys in school. Health care and education were free.

So, who paid for all that? Saddam Hussein did. But not willingly. A 2004 United Nations mandate known as the Oil-For-Food Programme sent 17 percent of Iraq's oil revenues to the Kurds, with no restrictions, part of the penalties imposed after the first Gulf War when the US and an international coalition severely spanked the Iraqi dictator for his ill-advised invasion of Kuwait. It was a boon to the northern reaches of the land once known as Mesopotamia, where writing, math, timekeeping, the calendar, astrology, and the code of law were first established.

Over the past decades, Saddam and his Baathist lackeys had prosecuted a relentless war of genocide against the Kurdish people, effectively destroying 4,000 of their 5,000 villages, denuding the landscape of almost every tree, eventually unleashing mustard gas attacks that killed up to 5,000 people in the first wave of bombings, and subsequently another 10,000 more through cancer and birth defects. The operation was dubbed *Al-Anfal*, which translates to "the spoils of war." The term also appears in the Quran's eighth sura, which describes the violent victory of 313 new Muslims over 900 non-Muslims in the battle of Badr in 624 AD. At that time, religious leaders assured the soldiers that taking cattle, goats, money, and women was religiously permitted. Saddam made the same declaration to his murderous soldiers. Morality, it seems, is a fungible commodity.

We traveled to the towns where we'd seen videos of men, women, and many, many children dying horribly in the streets, mucous pouring from their noses and mouths, gasping for breath as they clutched their swollen throats. We interviewed the family members of the massacred. We interviewed the chemical weapons experts who declared that the evidence of genocide was undeniable. We stood on a rocky riverbank and looked past the shoreline to the tanks that guarded Iraq's mainland and pondered whether those tanks, and worse, would soon be surging northward to kill even more innocent civilians.

The Kurds and their near-mythic guerrilla fighters, the Peshmerga, were determined to make sure that didn't happen.

A few days after our arrival, we got to see the Peshmerga up close as they trained. Alex and I ran through the hillsides with them as they practiced assault tactics, shooting live rounds. Many wore large tufts of grass or branches in their uniforms as camouflage as they ducked behind bushes to fire.

"Estimates are the Kurds can field about seventy thousand troops," I said in one on-camera stand-up for *Nightline*. "They have no heavy artillery, no armor, and no air force. Because of that, the question of whether they would fight alongside the US in another war against Saddam Hussein is a complicated one. Unlike the Northern Alliance in Afghanistan, they would not be fighting for the reconquest of their land. They would primarily be fighting for their own survival."

Saddam was their mortal enemy. But even so, siding with the US in that part of the world was an enormous risk. "Those who hate America, who cannot reach America," Masoud Barzani, leader of one of two Kurdish factions, told me, "they will direct their anger on us."

As we traveled through Kurdistan, we encountered one undeniable constant again and again: the people of Kurdistan, the women and children and working men, were not among "those who hate America." We could not have been more welcome. The appreciation for Western support of their endless struggle against the dictator to the south was palpable.

The stated purpose of the second war between the US and Iraq was the administration's claims that Saddam was in bed with al-Qaeda and somehow involved in, or tacitly supportive of, the 9/11 attacks, as well as being an on-going threat to

American national security. Secretary of State Colin Powell stood before the United Nations and claimed to have hard intelligence that Iraq possessed, and was ready to use, weapons of mass destruction.

"My colleagues, every statement I make today is backed up by sources, solid sources," he told the General Assembly. "These are not assertions. What we're giving you are facts and conclusions based on solid intelligence." The CIA insisted Saddam possessed "yellowcake"—a type of uranium powder that indicates, they assured Powell, that Iraq was well on the way to refining the radioactive element into U-235, the key element in nuclear weapons.

Two years later, the former secretary of state admitted he'd been duped by his own intelligence officers. "I'm the one who presented it on behalf of the United States to the world, and [it] will always be a part of my record. It was painful. It's painful now."

But was that the end of the story? Did Iraq really not have *any* weapons of mass destruction, or even the beginnings of the development of such? And even though Islamist scholars scoffed at the possibility that Saddam Hussein, a less-than-devout Sunni, would have joined common cause with al-Qaeda, a radical but extremely devout Shiite organization, was there really zero chance the two would join forces to damage the Great Satan, *America*, any way they could?

My stalwart crew and I traveled to a remote northern Iraq prison, where the Kurds were holding some men they told us were key to answering those questions. This is my verbatim "Reporter's Notebook" I filed for ABC's website. The full report, including the tense, incredible interviews with three prisoners, aired on *Nightline*.

YAMANIA, Iraq, Sept. 27, 2002—In a prison in the part of Northern Iraq controlled by Kurds, I sat down with three men who claim to have firsthand knowledge of links between Osama bin Laden's organization and Iraq.

The three men are in the custody of the Iraqi Kurdish government, which is opposed to Saddam Hussein's regime. All three assured me they were speaking of their own free will. They said they were not under threat of torture and they were aware they did not have to talk to me.

But prison interviews are always suspect because there's no way to know if they're exaggerating or simply lying in order to curry favor from their captors, and the information is difficult to confirm. All three men appeared to be calm and sincere, and their responses were very detailed, often including names and specific dates. Talking to me, they said, was a step towards righting the wrongs of their past.

'Trying to Assassinate American Journalists'

The first man sat before me with an Afghan scarf pulled up to just below his eyes. He asked not to be identified because he still has family in the area and feared for their safety. He said before his capture, he was a fighter for the radical militant Islamic group, Ansar al-Islam, that had been waging a small-scale insurgency against the Iraqi Kurdish government.

The United States and the Kurdish government believe Ansar al-Islam is directly linked to al Qaeda, and is part of a larger relationship between Saddam's regime and Osama bin Laden's terrorist organization.

According to this prisoner, there are about 500 to 600 men in the group, whose goals and methods were similar to the Taliban and al Qaeda. They want to institute a fundamentalist Islamic society and eventually control the entire region. According to him, al Qaeda is in fact, closely linked to Ansar al-Islam.

"Al Qaeda is a main finance source for al Ansar," he said, "because al Qaeda now doesn't have a particular base and is scattered. They only can provide financing to al Ansar. Definitely they have the same principles and goals, which the Taliban and al Qaeda have. Because [Ansar al-Islam] is in the early stage and they are small in size, they are not able to act against America as effectively as al Qaeda and Taliban did. But nevertheless, they don't hesitate to act against America. They do it, for example, they are trying to assassinate American journalists or kidnap them. Particularly those who come to Kurdistan."

That explained the heavily armed military escort the Kurdish government insisted we take with us on our visit to the front lines where Ansar al-Islam is active.

He went on to say that there were 80 al Qaeda fighters among Ansar al-Islam in the mountains of Northern Iraq at the time of his capture earlier this year.

Still, al Qaeda's influence with Ansar al-Islam is a far cry from the Bush administration's claims that bin Laden's organization is closely related to the Iraqi regime. But the next man I met said he had specific information about that.

Prisoner: Al Qaeda Members Met With Saddam

Abu Iman al-Maliki was convicted of spying on the Kurds as an Iraqi intelligence officer. He says he worked as such for 20 years. Al-Maliki chain-smoked Marlboros as we talked, sitting on a metal chair in a T-shirt advertising a martial arts school that strained against his bulk. He is, simply put, a huge man.

"The U.S. believes Iraq has had contact with al Qaeda," I said, "Do you know that to be a fact?"

"Yes. In '92, elements of al Qaeda came to Baghdad and met with Saddam Hussein and among them was Dr. Al-Zawahiri."

Ayman Al-Zawahiri, you may recall, has been identified as a top lieutenant of bin Laden's, and is widely thought to be a mastermind of the Sept. 11, 2001 attacks.

"There is a relationship between the governments of al Qaeda and the Iraqi government," he continued. "It began after the events of Kuwait approximately. That is when the relationship developed and many delegations came to Baghdad. There are elements of al Qaeda training on suicide operations, assassinations, explosions, and the making of chemical substances, and they are supervised by a number of officers, experts from the Iraqi intelligence, the Explosives Division, the Assassinations Division, different specialties."

Al-Maliki's specialty is somewhat more disturbing. He says he was part of a group of officers ordered by Saddam to hide chemical weapons throughout the Iraqi countryside. When I asked him if the U.N. weapons inspectors might find anything if they return, he smiled and said, "No. They will find nothing."

'I Killed' for Iraqi Intelligence and Al Qaeda

As midnight approached, I was introduced to Muhammad Mansour Shihab Ali, a man who, if you believe his confession, is a cold-hearted killer with a deep hatred for the United States.

His explanation of wanting to talk to an American journalist is the most perplexing of all: he had absolutely nothing to gain by doing so that I could tell. I asked him numerous times about his motives for giving us so much detailed information and his mumbled response, as gleaned by the translator, was that he thought I could do something to help his children whom he'd left behind with bin Laden's people in Afghanistan. It became obvious that he thought I was an American intelligence agent, and no amount of denial on my part could convince him otherwise.

Shihab Ali is in prison for the murder of an Iraqi dissident who had been living in Iran. He was captured at a Kurdish checkpoint and found in his possession were some photographic negatives which, when developed, were a full-color record of the grisly deed. When confronted in court with the photos, he confessed all. He's still confessing.

"Killing is something I did. I killed. This was for the Iraqi intelligence and al Qaeda."

Shihab Ali told me he has done numerous operations for al Qaeda and Iraq over the years, including numerous assassinations and smuggling drugs and guns. Two years ago, he says he was hired by an Iraqi intelligence officer, Othman Salman

Daoud, to smuggle 30 refrigerator "motors"—which I took to mean "compressors"—from Iraq to Iran, where they were handed over to men he describes as Afghan members of al Qaeda. He was paid $10,000 each for the items, which usually contain the refrigerant gas Freon, but, in this case, contained something more mysterious. Shihab Ali was warned it was dangerous to himself, and to any children he might hope to have.

We have no way of knowing what was in those compressors, or what their ultimate destination was. "Only God knows what was in them," he says. Which is not entirely true; he says the compressors were ordered by the man Shihab Ali met five days later in Afghanistan—bin Laden.

There were nine other operations he was expected to work on, he said, at the time he was caught, but he was reluctant to give away the details. Finally, I convinced him to tell me about one that was supposed to have happened last year. He says he and a partner were given $16 million to go to the Gulf and buy some large ships, equip them with 500 kilos of high explosive, and set sail under Iranian flags. The crews would slip away in motorboats after being replaced with men willing to commit suicide, who would then enter Kuwaiti waters, according to Shihab Ali, and ram the ships into American tankers or military vessels.

"The only reason this didn't happen is because you were captured?" I asked him as my mind filled with the mental image of the extent of death and damage such an attack might have caused.

"Yes, if I hadn't been arrested, I would have done it."

I left there hoping that his arrest had so compromised the operation, if indeed one had been planned at all, that it was scrapped.

I have no way of knowing how truthful these men were. Shihab Ali has been interviewed by print reporters in the past, one of whom described him as "deranged" because of his boasts of having killed so many people. After seeing the photographs of his last victim, I think that's an understandable assessment, although deranged in a Jeffrey Dahmer sort of way, not as a raving lunatic. As he sat there, quietly and methodically describing his experiences, I couldn't help but think he was capable of everything he was saying.

If I was sitting in the same room listening to the same man last Sept. 10, I'm not sure I would have believed a word he said.

CHAPTER 41

SQUARED AWAY

Reporter's Notebook, ABCNews.com, March 26, 2003.

His cot is across the tent from mine. As I look at it now, every camouflage green bag containing Army-issue clothes and Army-issue ammunition and Army-issue gadgets is neatly zipped, strapped, and stacked. His towel hangs perfectly straight from a cord stretched overhead. His sleeping bag is rolled up to keep the scorpions out.

Sgt. Maj. Jim Clinton's billet is, as he would say, squared away. Roger that.

His life has been the Army. Ask to see a picture of his wife and he pulls out a frayed photograph from when he made First Sergeant. He's in dress blues, at attention, arm and chest a crayon-box of colored ribbons and stripes. The pretty woman next to him smiles shyly in contrast to his stern, slightly uncomfortable frown, as if sergeants aren't allowed to smile in public.

The face in the picture is a little less crinkly than the one I see now. The scalp a little more covered. His face reminds me of the WWII cartoons by Bill Mauldin, the ones about the two GIs. Tough, haggard, all ears and jaw and stubble.

They got married the day before he joined up. Twenty-five years ago. He still shouts with joy when he gets a letter from her, like yesterday. He leaned over and waved it in my face playfully. "She wants my body," he growls in a voice made sandpaper rough from decades of Marlboros and shouting at grunts. He points to the printed address label. "Made up a hundred of these before I left. Put a hundred stamps on 'em. Now all she has to do is jot down 'I love you' on a piece of paper, stick it in the mail, and she's made my day."

The fact that he was busy reading that letter for 20 minutes makes me think she wrote a little more than that.

Sgt. Clinton will take the time to patiently describe in detail to a novice how to fieldstrip an M-4 rifle. He will tell big, long, circuitous war stories that don't always end up where they started off for. He will make sure you're drinking enough water and brushing your teeth, because after a few dozen years of not being so diligent himself, the Army had to fit him with quite a few new ones.

And with a frightful blast of spittle and roar he will pin back the ears of any enlisted man who doesn't jump to his "gentle" suggestions.

In the morning he moves like his joints are put on backwards. A life of sleeping on the ground and jumping over things and diving under things and hauling twice your body weight over distant miles will do that to you. He unfolds slowly, like an origami figure coming apart.

His mother was a Czechoslovakian who came to America with no money and no contacts after her father had been forcibly conscripted into the German Army during WWII and sent to the Russian front. He didn't survive long. Somehow, she made it out of Europe. Somehow, she learned English on her own and learned a skill and built a family.

The sergeant major says he thinks of her often, especially now, out here, because she's one of the reasons he joined the Army. One of the reasons he loves the Army. "I guess because of what she went through," he says, struggling for words. "What America meant to her, and what we are here to protect. Freedom."

Clinton has a weakness for Pringles. He washes his clothes in a garbage bag rather than wait for the four-day camp laundry service. The Bowie-knife angles of his craggy face are dulled a bit by the bifocals he's now forced to wear.

And inside his Army-issue flak jacket, wrapped around the ceramic plate that protects his heart, is a full-sized American flag.

CHAPTER 42

A MOST GLAMOROUS PROFESSION

Twenty hours into the invasion of Iraq, and I had to go number two. Badly. Bouncing along in the back of an up-armored Humvee had jostled the highly caloric MRE from the night before completely through my lower intestines, and everything not distributed to various cells was screaming that the party was over and that it was waiting at the back door and needed to leave. When the US Army unit I was traveling with finally stopped at a temporary desert staging point, I saw my opportunity.

"Hi," I called out to a soldier walking by, "where's the latrine?"

"Ain't one. We're not staying here long enough to dig one."

I looked around. There was no gas station, of course, no Starbucks, no rest stop, not even a disgusting porta-potty. Just flat, featureless desert and a few thousand grunts walking around, waiting for orders. Ah, yes. One of the many glamorous things about covering hurricanes, earthquakes, blizzards, and wars: finding somewhere to go to the bathroom.

The disturbance in my lower abdomen was becoming acute. I couldn't wait any longer. Pulling out the rain poncho from my pack and the travel-sized roll of toilet paper, I walked as far as I could from the collection of vehicles and soldiers, dug a hole in the sand, slipped on the poncho, dropped trou, and set about doing my business.

I was almost finished when a Deuce and a Half truck rolled by with a dozen soldiers in the back. A few took notice of the solitary figure squatting out in the open with his head poking out from a tiny plastic tent. There could be no question what I was doing. In the midst of scattered laughter, one of them stood up and pointed.

"Hey!" he shouted. "Aren't you that guy on TV?"

CHAPTER 43

AMBUSH AT THE ALAMO

April 2003. Somewhere near Najaf, Iraq. We'd been pushing steadily northward for weeks, with our unit meeting sporadic resistance from Saddam's holdouts harassing convoys along the way. Being embedded meant journalists did not have our own vehicles (with the exception of some notable anchors like David Bloom and Ted Koppel), so we had to squeeze ourselves into any military method of conveyance that had the space. To save room on that particular trip, I was carrying only my camera gear, my satellite transmission equipment, and a small personal bag of water, food, and medical supplies. My larger kit, including my heavy coat and sleeping bag, was with ABC News producer Jay Weiss, traveling a different route. Every damn night I regretted not having that kit as I lay shivering on the sand or on top of a truck hood, looking up at the stars, trying to sleep in the freezing winter temperatures. The occasional ground-shaking thumps and orange glows on the horizon spoke of the artillery assaults by the Third Infantry Division being carried out just ahead of us.

Traveling at night in blackout conditions presented its own dangers. A few days earlier, I was hitching a ride in a Humvee with the 318th PSYOP Company, which sported a huge loudspeaker on its roof. The team, Kurt, Tim, and Cherie (they asked that I not use their last names or ranks), would ordinarily be blaring messages to the hidden Iraqis to surrender or face certain death, but this night we were rolling along in silence when the vehicle slammed into a sand dune that had blown partially across the road during one of the frequent windstorms. No one was injured, but the engine belts and water pump were destroyed. As the team awaited a tow, I opted to climb into an open-air supply truck that paused just long enough to see if everyone was OK. I needed to catch up with the rest of Bruch's men to chronicle whatever they were finding ahead. Huddled as I was in the bed of the truck, arms wrapped around my chest, teeth chattering, it's a miracle I didn't get frostbite on that ride north. As we slowly bumped along the bomb-scarred highway, I could see dozens of destroyed Iraqi vehicles and bodies littering the roadside. Through my night vision scope they appeared eerily green, almost inhuman, as if they were movie props. But these were not manikins. Over a thousand Iraqi soldiers died in this small area alone.

The group I was officially embedded with, 2/502 Strike Force, a battalion with the 101st Airborne out of Fort Campbell, Kentucky, was tasked with rearguard cleanup after the armored division rolled through. Along the way we ducked regular potshots from snipers and had to pick our way through numerous minefields. Clearing the buildings was a slow, dangerous, and occasionally exceedingly violent process. After Strike Force set up its Tactical Operations Center, or TOC, at an abandoned school, Lt. Col. Bruch sent a few squads out for reconnaissance. Bruch gave the OK for me to join Charlie Company as they headed off on foot toward a neighborhood of apartments and industrial sites.

These soldiers were young—primarily in their twenties, impressively fit, and well trained. They ran across open fields, jumped barbed-wire fences, and kicked in metal doors. I kept up with them as best I could, hauling camera gear, extra batteries, and my BGAN satellite transmitter in a backpack.

Small satellite phones like the Thuraya or Iridium were not yet capable of sending large video files.

The BGAN was transformative for those of us covering the war. It allowed us to report live, albeit with the jerky *Max Headroom*-type low-resolution transmissions, and feed our edited pieces back to ABC headquarters for air. It required quite a bit of technical setup, though, to get its three folding panels (the "dish") lined up perfectly with a specific satellite. The *New York Times* profiled us in a March 24, 2003, article on how new technology was bringing the war home to American viewers:

> Informed by the military that their two-member "embedded" teams would be able to take only the equipment they could personally carry, many television news operations have provided their reporters with a compact kit—one that enables them to capture, edit, compress and send video with a small digital camera, a laptop computer and a satellite phone.
>
> For Don Dahler and Jay Weiss of ABC News, that means the ability to travel anywhere with the 101st Airborne Division, currently in Kuwait. A profile the two produced on Thursday of the day in the life of a sniper was broadcast on Friday. The technology is turning reporters and camera operators into producers and editors, making often painful judgments about what to include.
>
> Their two-and-a-half minute piece took four hours to compress and send. But the video quality from such setups is good, and the reporting can get quickly out to the world.

"The fact that we can file stories at all without a dish or having access to a dish is stunning to me," said Mr. Dahler, who had envisioned delays of days or even weeks when he first learned of the conditions of being placed with a unit. "We have made a quantum leap in our ability to conduct journalism," he said in a telephone interview.

But the conducting of said journalism was still risky, exhausting, and subject to strict rules handed down by the Pentagon, which included never revealing a unit's position—we could only use general descriptions—and never showing dead or injured Americans. I didn't object to either condition. The former was for everyone's safety, including journalists, and the latter was out of sensitivity to family members who may not yet have been notified.

A certain mustachioed Fox News reporter, known for his oversized ego and self-aggrandizing exaggerations, was summarily kicked out of Iraq by the US Army for violating the first restriction. Geraldo Rivera, embedded with a different 101st Airborne unit than I, was broadcasting live when he drew a map in the sand pinpointing the unit's exact location near Baghdad while revealing the particulars, including the time, of a scheduled assault. This is the same "journalist" who, two years earlier, claimed to have been at the scene of a deadly friendly fire incident in Kandahar, Afghanistan, where three American soldiers were killed and who emotionally described himself as having stood on "hallowed ground" while saying the Lord's Prayer over the plot of land where the soldiers had fallen. Problem is that the event he was talking about actually happened three hundred miles away from where he was doing his live shot at Tora Bora. When confronted about this discrepancy by NPR's David Folkenflik, Rivera claimed the fog of war caused him confusion as to where the incident took place, and that he was referring to a friendly fire incident in

Tora Bora. Reasonable explanation, perhaps, if you hold your head just so and squint, except the tragedy he was then referring to didn't actually happen until four days *after* his "hallowed ground" report. Never let the facts get in the way of a good story, I guess. Rivera denies it to this day; Folkenflik stands by his reporting.

My commitment to the second issue, not naming or showing injured and dead soldiers, was tested on April 7, when the unit air assaulted the outskirts of Karbala. We loaded into some Chinook helicopters, which took off and flew very fast and low over the ground, popping off flares and chaff along the way to deter any surface to air missiles. When we all disembarked and the choppers took off again, we found ourselves walking through an enormous minefield. The shiny little pointed triggers were visible sticking out of the ground every twenty feet or so, arranged in a grid. The soldiers passed the word back man to man: "Step only in the footprints ahead of you." Some of the men carried little flagsticks to mark the explosives for demolition.

Before all of us made it out of the minefield, we heard a large explosion. One of Delta Company's Humvees had hit an improvised explosive device (IED) closer to the edge of town. As the truck burned, the extra ammunition in the back began popping off. Despite the danger, a sergeant by the name of O'Shea (I only know that because of his name tag—he refused to tell me his first name or be interviewed when I spoke to him later) drove up next to the damaged vehicle and pulled the badly injured driver out. He then ordered the gunner on top of his Humvee to "clear a path"—firing the Mk 19 grenade launcher into the ground directly in front of them to detonate any other IEDs. My footage of the incident shows the vehicle creeping forward with the regular *pok...boom, pok...boom* of the big gun. The vehicle made it back to safe ground, and the wounded soldier was medevacked by chopper. As soon as I could set up my satellite system, I reported on the incident and explained that the soldier was still alive but fighting for his life.

Here's what I couldn't report: his name. Even though, by that time, I knew it. It was Jose Rene Martinez, a twenty-year-old infantryman from Shreveport, Louisiana, who enlisted almost a year to the day after the 9/11 attacks. J.R., as he was known, was one of the most popular guys in his unit, described to me as always smiling and joking.

In the IED explosion, J.R. suffered burns over 34 percent of his body and severe smoke inhalation. The burn experts at Ramstein Air Base in Germany saved his life, and the surgeons at Brooke Army Medical Center in San Antonio conducted over thirty plastic surgeries and skin grafts to rebuild his damaged face and body.

You may remember hearing about J.R. Martinez. He went on to become a successful actor on *All My Children* and won Season 13 of *Dancing with the Stars*. He is also an in-demand motivational speaker, for good reason.

Anyway, back to running and ducking and crawling through disgusting sewage ditches with Charlie Company. As I videotaped them fighting and interrogating and searching the seemingly endless buildings outside Najaf, it was brought home to me, and hopefully our viewers, just how tough their job was, and how tough these men were. My scribbled, somewhat hurried journal entries from those days describe them finding stockpiles of weapons hidden in homes, rocket-propelled grenades (RPGs) stored inside a Mercedes, more RPGs in a mosque, and a bomb-making factory inside a technical school, both of the latter in clear violation of the Geneva Convention. Alpha Company took two enemy prisoners of war. And Delta Company located what they strongly suspected was a cache of chemical weapons. Yep. Those nasty little weapons of mass destruction that the prisoner in Kurdistan told me the inspectors would never find and that the US government eventually declared didn't exist after all.

I happened to be at the TOC the day that radio call came in from Delta, nursing an injured Achilles I'd blown out trying to jump over a fence during a hair-raising, bullets-flying assault by Charlie Company on a house. Because they were in the middle of a firefight, the young officer understandably couldn't spare anyone to evacuate me from the area, so I hobbled a few miles through "enemy territory" back to the abandoned school where Strike Force was bivouacked. Doc Cranston, the former Special Forces medic and beloved raconteur, gave me a steroid and painkiller shot directly into the tendon. That was exceedingly pleasant, sort of a cross between someone driving a nail into my heel and being hit by a bolt of lightning. But after a few moments the agony subsided somewhat. When I tested my weight on it, my ankle felt crunchy, but bearable.

Lt. Col. Bruch ordered Delta to back off and stay a safe distance from the site while maintaining security. He grabbed his Kevlar, and he and a few others started out the door.

"Colonel!" I shouted after him. "Mind if I come along?"

He looked me up and down, his gaze lingering for a moment on my newly wrapped ankle. "You sure you're up for it?"

I pulled on my boot. I had to loosen the laces all the way to fit it over the wrapping. "If they really did find WMDs, you'll want video. And I want the story."

He nodded. I grabbed my camera and limped to the Humvee.

The site in question was located next to the Euphrates River in a town named Albu Aziz, between Karbala and Hillah. I seem to recall it took us about an hour to reach it. The company commander, Capt. Kenneth Hutchison, had deployed his soldiers at a safe distance around the bridge, which they discovered to be rigged with explosives. They were under strict orders to keep all locals away.

Capt. Hutchison, whom everyone his rank or above called Hutch, led us around a building and down a slight hill to where we could see a Quonset hut sitting in someone's back-yard. Multiple colored wires were visible leading out of the building's open door, and inside we could see numerous large blue barrels.

"Looks like a terrorist training camp," Hutch told his colonel, pointing to the other buildings. "No one inside but lots of instructional materials, documents, weapons."

"Do we know what's in the barrels?" Col. Bruch asked.

"Our CW kicked off positive," he replied. That was the chemical weapons sensor every unit carried. It could "sniff" the air and detect various kinds of toxins, even below levels considered nonthreatening. Hutch handed Bruch his binoculars. "If you look inside the door, I think those are explosives rigged next to the barrels."

That was all Bruch needed to hear. He radioed for a Chemical Corps team and Explosive Ordnance Disposal unit to be dispatched, and as I shot video of the site, he ordered Delta to maintain a perimeter. "Nobody goes near that shed," he told Hutch. "Especially not a civilian. Stay here until the CW guys arrive."

Before we left the location, I made a quick radio report via my Thuraya sat phone, carefully describing what we were seeing but avoiding any conclusions or hyperbole (or specific location). I fully intended to stay on the story.

A few days later, Lt. Col. Bruch told me the chem team hadn't found any weapons-grade materials in those barrels. I looked at him in surprise. "Then what was there, and why the explosives? Why rig the bridge?"

He just shrugged. After having spent the better part of a month with the man, I could tell when he knew something he couldn't or wouldn't tell me. I never did find out what was in that building. But it was damn suspicious.

One thing you learn quickly after spending time with the US Military is just how impressive the technology is that they can bring to bear in combat. A unit on the ground, like

Charlie Company, is never truly alone. There are often eyes in the sky, both illuminating and lethal. I remember watching an A-10 Warthog open up its 30 mm autocannon on a concrete bunker from which Iraqi snipers had been pinning down nearby troops. The huge rounds completely annihilated the structure within seconds. Anyone inside was undoubtedly reduced to little more than hamburger and ketchup.

Officers at the point of the spear, such as Maj. Kunk and Lt. Col. Bruch, are briefed multiple times a day by their intelligence officers, who get the latest battlefield assessments on an almost instantaneous basis. I wasn't privy to all of these, but I witnessed enough to conclude the Americans had eyes on pretty much everything the Iraqi army was up to.

Sometimes, however, those assessments were dead wrong. Such as the day of the Ambush at the Alamo.

It was the beginning of spring. The winter chill had finally retreated, and in its stead was a sudden onslaught of desert heat. One journal entry notes my watch was showing ninety-six degrees in the shade. I took part in what was supposed to be a routine recon mission through the fringes of Najaf, which quickly turned into a full-scale running battle. I was in a Humvee with a sniper/scout team and Bruch was in the vehicle just ahead of us when the bullets started flying. He immediately ordered his soldiers to set up emplacements near a bridge, and they began pushing forward, avoiding the homemade landmines haphazardly strewn on the ground. It took hours, but the 2/502 ultimately cleared all the government buildings from which the Iraqis were firing, and we returned to the abandoned school that had become the unit's command center. Fatigued, dirty, and hungry, I was just getting ready to tuck into my spaghetti-and-meatballs MRE when I caught Maj. Kunk's eye as he was heading into the tactical center, the room where the officers worked and all the high-tech communications equipment resided. "You might want to hear this," he said. "No camera."

Lt. Col. Bruch was inside, already receiving a briefing from one of the intelligence officers. He glanced over and motioned me with his head to take a spot near the wall of maps. It took me a moment to piece together what the issue was, mainly because I had to mentally decipher all the acronyms being tossed around, but eventually I figured it out. We were in deep trouble.

A typical Army battalion has between three hundred and one thousand soldiers, but per embed regulations, the specific number of people under Bruch's direct command was confidential. Understandable, considering any broadcast reports of actual troop strength would be beneficial to the Iraqis. That's only pertinent in this context because of what the intel from J-STARS was saying that day, namely, that two large columns of Iraqi mechanized forces were on the move south, on the very road that ran right next to the school in which we were standing. That meant that armored vehicles, possibly even T-72 tanks, and thousands of soldiers would be on top of the 2/502 in a matter of hours.

J-STARS, by the way, is Pentagon jargon for Joint Surveillance Target Attack Radar System, a high-tech airborne surveillance, battle management, and command-and-control platform married to a modified Boeing 707-300 and operated by the US Air Force. It flies above the battlefield, watching troop movements, listening in on enemy communications, and directing fire, either from artillery or attack aircraft, among other things.

Bruch declared, in his calm, professorial way, that their orders were to stop or at least slow down the Iraqis until the Third Infantry Division's armored brigade could get there. One of the officers next to me (I think it was Maj. Jim Shaver) leaned over and whispered, "Welcome to the Alamo." If the intelligence was correct, Strike Force would face a much superior force, outmanned and outgunned.

This was one of those moments when I couldn't dial up ABC on my Thuraya and report what was going on because that would tip off the Iraqis that the Americans knew they were coming and give them at least a clue as to what might be waiting for them. For operational security, I couldn't even call Katie to tell her I loved her. So, instead, I set about preparing to cover the coming battle as best I could.

I set up my two small video cameras on their miniature tripods at strategic corners of the roof to give different angles of the fighting. My plan was to quickly turn them on to run automatically when the fighting started and then station myself with the sniper team overlooking the road, filming the action with my main camera. The 2/502 scout/snipers carried one of the most lethal weapons on earth—the Barrett M82, a large, heavy rifle that fired an enormous 0.50 caliber round. Those cartridges are powerful enough to travel over a mile with accuracy and packed enough punch to disable a car engine or, depending on the type of bullet, pierce armor. You don't want to picture what they'd do to the human body. I'd been out with that team before, and I figured that, barring a direct hit on us from a tank shell, those guys were going to inflict some serious damage.

Below us, I watched as Delta Company positioned its Humvees with the Mk 19 grenade launchers behind trees and other obstacles. Delta was also equipped with the battalion's Javelin shoulder-fired antiarmor missiles, and Hutch placed some of his tank-buster teams on either side of the road in an ambush formation. I don't know how many Javelin munitions they had, but my guess was not nearly enough to knock out an entire armored column. When I asked one of the officers, he explained that the plan was to kill as many of the lead vehicles as possible in the first moments of battle, so as to create a logjam. Then, when the tanks tried to maneuver down the adjoining streets, they'd knock them out to block those points of egress as well, stalling the advance long enough for the cavalry to arrive.

Meanwhile, the rest of the 2/502 were preparing fighting positions in the building's windows and behind concrete walls. I don't know what the soldiers were really thinking, but I saw no panic, no nervousness, just steel-jawed professionalism. Not to resort to jingoism here, but I've never witnessed a better representation of the quality training the young men and women of the US Armed Forces receive. Every one of them knew what they were facing. And every one of them was prepared to do the job. Regardless of whether you think the Iraq war was justified, I think you'd be proud of these people if you saw them go about their business that day. I know I was.

Finally, the preparations were complete, and we all hunkered down in our positions to wait it out. Maj. Kunk was making his rounds, checking on everyone, and as he squatted down next to me, he patted my shoulder. I can't remember his exact words, delivered in that magnificent baritone, but it was something to the effect of: "This might be one of those moments we talked about. If things go south, you might have to put down that camera and pick up a weapon." I assured him I would. While thinking that, if that moment did arrive, we'd all be screwed.

Minutes went by. Then hours. I didn't dare risk going back down to the tactical center to see what was happening for fear I'd be out of position when it kicked off. But just before sunset the word spread to stand down. There would be no attack. The soldiers of Strike Force stood up, stretched, and began whatever their normal duties were, because a soldier's work is rarely done. But they did so with evident relief on their faces.

Bruch explained later, with a wry smile, that either the intel was bad, or the Iraqis simply decided to abandon their move south. We, at the Alamo, had been ready. But this time, Generalissimo Santa Anna was a no-show.

CHAPTER 44

THAT TIME I ALMOST
HAD TO KILL A GUY

Two hours into the drive, the bearded man sitting next to me casually mentioned in halting English that President Saddam Hussein was offering $50,000 for any captured American soldier, dead or alive. He was cradling an ancient AK-47 in his lap as he said it. I couldn't read his smile. Malevolent or kidding? Regardless, I didn't want my next television appearance to be on Iraqi TV as the latest high-profile hostage. I slipped my six-inch knife out of my pocket and held it out of sight.

I couldn't blame him for mistaking me for a soldier. I was clothed head-to-foot in US Army–issued desert camouflage, complete with Kevlar ballistic vest and the dusty K-pot helmet bearing my name and blood type. As a journalist embedded with the 101st Airborne, the theory went that it was safer to not wear civilian clothing in the combat zone, as Iraqi snipers would assume anyone doing so was CIA and thus a much more appealing target. It also made my fashion decisions much easier during the three months I spent with the Screaming Eagles as they methodically made their way from Kuwait toward Baghdad. The whole question of Louboutin pumps or Jimmy Choo flats was moot at that point. Heavy-soled beige army boots were the only footwear option available.

When we first met on a bomb-cratered street in a small town just north of the larger city of Samawah, he told me his name was Jasim Madlool, a veteran of Iraq's disastrous war with Iran, which ended over a decade ago. He showed me a few puckered scars on his stomach from those good times in Saddam's army. "*Bang bang*," he chuckled, making the universal sign of pulling a trigger with his finger. It was then I noticed a fresher injury on his side, with a large grimy bandage and orange-brown stains from an apparently still fresh wound. I motioned to it. He responded vaguely in a mishmash of Arabic and English. I never quite got the context. But I was hoping it was the result of an unfortunate nail clipper accident, as opposed to a confrontation with the American military.

Jasim was among a crowd of other equally hirsute observers standing around me and my little Nissan pickup truck next to a fountain in the middle of what military intelligence called "Shialand." Micro history lesson: Saddam was a Sunni. He and most Sunni Muslims hate Shias. The feeling is mutual. Sunnis are by far the largest Islamic sect in the world; the Shia are the majority in but a few nations, including Iran and, ironically, Iraq. The Islamic schism, as historians call it, dates back to an internecine fight between the prophet Muhammad's relatives about who would succeed the prophet—his father-in-law or his son-in-law. Saddam, as president of Iraq, had considerable influence over the country's Shia population. And by *influence* I mean that he could still kill them all.

By the way, the fountain wasn't working. Neither was the truck.

It was a gift from Lt. Col. Stephen Bruch, commanding officer of the 2/502 out of Fort Campbell, Kentucky, the unit I'd been attached to since early March. The red Nissan had been confiscated from an Iraqi officer, who'd wisely surrendered rather than take on the 101st, which hadn't ended so well for a large number of his contemporaries. Bruch's soldiers had been slogging through Iraq on a cleanup mission, following on the heels of the Third Infantry Division, which was sweeping north at breakneck speed. The larger armored units moved so fast that pockets of Iraqi military were passed by as they huddled in schools and basements and desert wadis waiting for the initial assault to die down. Those were the people the Strike Force brigade was after. It was hard, dirty, dangerous business—kicking in doors, running gun battles street to street, scanning windows for snipers, sweeping roads for mines, dodging IEDs.

I'd barely arrived in Kuwait when my wife, Katie, joyously informed me in a satellite phone call that she was pregnant with our first child. Great timing on my part, right? So, after over four weeks covering the buildup of American forces in Kuwait and the ultimate invasion of Iraq for ABC News, and with the 2/502 staying put in the Najaf area for at least a short period, I decided it was a good time to get my tail home. Some priorities are crystal clear. Husband gone during entire crucial first trimester of pregnancy—bad. Husband stays alive in war and comes home to rub achy back and feet of pregnant wife—good. My plan was to spend a few weeks with her before rejoining the unit at a later date.

When I first broached the subject of leaving with Lt. Col. Bruch a few days earlier, he suggested Doc Cranston ride along with me so that he could load up with medicine and supplies in Kuwait City. William "Wild Bill" Cranston was former Special Forces who'd gone to Army physician's assistant school, achieved the rank of warrant officer, and was reassigned to the 2/502. At least, that was the official story. In my experience, those SF guys are as mysterious as they come, trained to play four-dimensional chess amid a three-dimensional war. The people who make it into Special Forces aren't only the stereotypical Rambo-types. They're selected for their brains, their ability to work in the shadows, their skills with languages and other cultures, counterintelligence, counterinsurgency, and their on-the-fly creativity. They also often have an independent streak. Cranston was, in the words of one of the officers who oversaw him, a "cowboy." While we were still in Kuwait waiting for the war to begin, Doc would occasionally show up at our tent with forged passes, which allowed us to visit the Starbucks in Kuwait City (and, uh, other places) despite a strict base lockdown. My kinda guy. If the Army statute of limitations hasn't expired for that behavior, I will state for the record that I just told a fib. Doc never did any such thing (*wink, wink*). Repeat after me: "Wild Bill Cranston is the kindest, bravest, warmest, most wonderful human being I've ever known in my life." (By the way: The Frank Sinatra version of *The Manchurian Candidate* was better than Denzel's. And I love Denzel.)

Back to our story. Suddenly word came that the unit's pause-in-place was rescinded, and they were to start another hard push northward. Bruch decided he couldn't risk losing Doc even for just a few days. A sergeant whose mother was gravely ill back in Kentucky volunteered to take his place, but the Army's mountain of red tape buried that idea fifty feet deep. I'd already told Katie I was coming out, so I had to decide whether to make the trip on my own or wait for God knows how long before I could get a ride or flight back to the promised land.

I chose the former. Go ahead and say it. I'm an idiot. This is probably not the last time you'll draw that conclusion.

The colonel had his men load up the back of the truck with a large drum of gasoline, bottles of water, some sickeningly sweet Iraqi Kufa Colas, and a case of MREs (military-issue meals ready to eat). These MREs were the new version, with just-add-water chemical heat packs and little bags of M&M's—1,250 calories of questionably healthy goodness. Spaghetti or beef stew seemed to be the hands-down favorites among the grunts. Chicken with egg noodles was the least. Bruch gave me a handwritten document to produce if and when I came in contact with other military units, requesting they grant me "freedom of movement" and that I be treated with "the respect and dignity of a field grade officer in the rank of Major."

I added my three duffle bags to the mix: one containing a change of clothes, a coat, knit cap (it gets damn cold in the desert at night), and various toiletries; the other my sleeping bag, rain tarp, and MOPP gear (Mission Oriented Protective Posture), which included a gas mask and a full-body nuclear, biological, and chemical suit. We wore those damn things for two full weeks at the start of the invasion during repeated Scud attacks by Iraq's president. The body odor created by a tent full of athletic male bodies sweating all day inside individual ziplock bags is eye-watering torture. Waterboarding pales in comparison. The third reinforced canvas bag held the hundred pounds of video and satellite transmission gear and spare batteries I'd been hauling around for the better part of a month.

As I heaved the last bag into the bed of the truck, Col. Bruch approached and held out his hand. In it was a 9 mm semiautomatic pistol.

"I can't accept that," I said.

"Take it. This is a war zone. We won't be there to protect you."

The gun was one Bruch had personally relieved from a surrendering Iraqi officer a few days earlier. It was in perfect condition. He made it clear he wanted it back after the war was over, likely for Fort Campbell's museum, but in his judgment I'd be insane to go off alone and unarmed. By law he couldn't issue me a US Army weapon, so this was the best solution he could come up with.

I should state here that Stephen Bruch is one of the smartest guys you'd ever meet. Degrees in physics from West Point and UVA. A deeply religious man, he was respected by his soldiers for hitting the gym and the running track with them every day, even before the war. He told me he couldn't expect his twenty-something-old enlistees to do anything he wasn't willing to do. Bruch had easily ten years on most of his soldiers, but he regularly won the base pull-up contests.

I should also state here that I'm in no way afraid of firearms. I own them. I've been trained by various police offices and military experts in their use over the years. I've fired pretty much anything you can imagine. And I'm a pretty good shot.

But one of the first things I was required to do when I volunteered to be embedded in the US Army was sign a document saying that I, as a noncombatant, would not carry a weapon. Period. Full stop. It's a stricture that dates back to the Geneva Convention. The Pentagon did not want gung ho journalists getting involved in combat, no matter how enthusiastic certain TV personalities were about the prospect of bagging Saddam themselves (I'm looking at you, Geraldo).

Although, full confession, as the unit was preparing to head into Iraq, Major Tom Kunk, the towering six-foot-six executive officer nicknamed "Bald Eagle," perhaps because he was, in fact, bald and patriotic as hell, pulled me aside and zeroed his intimidating gaze into my eyes.

"I'm not sure about this whole embedding thing. We usually see reporters as more trouble than benefit. Most of you guys don't know anything about the military. But I need to know, if we take you into our family, if we trust you, I need to know if things get dicey, you'll drop your camera and pick up a weapon. I need to know that. We all need to trust that you'll have our backs when we have yours. Because this can get very real very fast. Those bullets start flying, you have to pick a side."

I assured him I would. I meant it. And there was one time I almost had to make good on it. I'll tell you about that later.

Kunk nodded solemnly and announced to all in his booming voice, "From now on, your call sign is Captain America. He's one of us, boys. Welcome to Strike Force." Kunk saw it as his job to give everyone their nickname. They always stuck.

But *Captain America*????

There was a chorus of "hooahs" from the soldiers in the tent. I'm not sure I've ever been more honored.

Fast-forward to the little red pickup weaving its way through destroyed vehicles and pocked roads on my way back to Kuwait. Captain America had a bit of confusion trying to find his way through the town of Karbala, as all the street signs were in Arabic, but by following the waypoints I'd marked in my handheld GPS when the 2/502 first passed this way (this was before smartphones), I managed to backtrack through the urban areas and locate the main road again.

It was all going so well for most of that first day. Until it wasn't.

I'd been chugging along at one hundred kilometers per hour, listening to scratchy rock 'n' roll on bootleg radio stations at the farthest end of the dial, when the engine began to sputter, then quit altogether. I coasted to a stop next to the dried-up fountain and got out to see what I could see. My inconspicuous garb attracted immediate attention. A crowd of curious onlookers, mostly berobed men with copious beards holding AK-47s, gathered around, chattering in Arabic. That's when Jasim stepped up and introduced himself. He knew a smattering of English, so our communication was mainly in the form of random words and hand signals.

After poking around under the hood, I concluded there was probably water in the gasoline. I have a little mechanical ability, having been employed at an oil change and tune-up franchise in high school and helped my dad rebuild a Model A and old Dodge truck as a kid. Had I been back in the US, I would've drained the gas tank, blown out the fuel lines, and filled it back up with unleaded. Bing bang boom, merrily, merrily on my way. On a street in the middle of Iraq, that wasn't going to happen.

I would've paid a small fortune for a ride across the border. But there were no Ubers to call. Not even a taxi in sight. I sat down on the side of the fountain, popped open a Kufa Cola, and offered one to Jasim. He accepted it with a grin and sat down next to me. Dozens of curious faces looked on intently. Any one of them could've been one of Saddam's lackeys in civilian clothing, but there was nothing I could do about that. Besides, I figured, most of these folks probably had loved ones murdered by their own country's president. *The enemy of my enemy...*

Jasim pointed to my own clothes and then gestured toward the horizon. "Americans," he said. I didn't catch on at first, so he repeated it. Then I got it. He was telling me there were other American soldiers that way. I nodded.

He then turned to a man standing next to us and said something to him. The man quickly disappeared for a few moments, then returned driving a beat-up sedan.

I wasn't willing to give up on the Nissan, just in case we did run into a military unit that could help me get it running again, so I fished around in my pack for some 550 cord—a thin yet super-strong Army rope—and together we wound it around the two vehicles' bumpers multiple times to create a towrope.

Jasim hopped into the passenger seat of the pickup, and a few of his buddies, all armed, jumped into the sedan. The sea of spectators parted, and we slowly pulled away from the fountain, hoping against hope the makeshift towrope wouldn't break.

As we rolled along, I placed a satellite phone call to ABC News. I wasn't kidding myself. There would be no rescue team coming to find me if I suddenly disappeared, not in the middle of a war, but at least they'd know what had happened. I reported my general location, situation, and aspiration. Michael Kreisel, who was manning the foreign desk back in New York at the time, didn't quite know what to say, other than: "Good luck."

Our two-car caravan ventured farther and farther into the desert. Jasim used every English word he knew to keep the conversation alive. I smiled and nodded as if I understood what the hell he was talking about. But the miles kept going by, and there was still no sign of other Americans. An hour passed and I asked him, "Americans?" and gestured ahead. He nodded emphatically. That's when he showed me his bullet scars and told me about Saddam's offer, and the unpleasant thought came to mind that it was a setup; that he and his friends were taking me to the Iraqi army instead to collect their reward.

I slipped the knife out and held it against my thigh as I began working up a plan to take his rifle away. I knew even if I succeeded doing that it was still one against four. But I figured if I was captured, I'd be tortured and killed anyway, maybe in a very public, very horrible way, so my options were limited. The thought occurred, more than once, that that damn 9 mm would've come in really handy about now.

At that exact moment—no kidding; right then—the driver of the sedan began honking his horn and slowed to a stop just as we crested a rise in the road. Beyond him stretched a line of a dozen armored vehicles headed our way.

US Army armored vehicles.

Saved by the cavalry. Literally. It was a patrol from the Second Cavalry Regiment. I slid the knife back into its sheath.

There was, of course, still a war going on. So the nice gentlemen from Hawk Company pointed their weapons at us and ordered us in very scary, loud voices to lie flat on the ground as they patted down every inch of our bodies and took a good look in the vehicles. When I finally had the chance, I explained who I was and what I was doing there to an incredulous Maj. Ward, who no doubt concluded I was the dumbest (and luckiest) man that side of the Euphrates River.

"Where you headed?" he asked.

"Kuwait. How about you?"

"Najaf."

My heart sank. "I just came from there."

"Looks like you're going back," motioning toward my disabled truck, "unless you want to keep taking your chances with these fellas."

"No thanks. I've had enough fun today."

Jasim's eyes filled with tears as we said our goodbyes. Not because of any affection for me—I had just handed him the keys to the Nissan and a handful of money. That car was worth more than he'd make for years to come. I passed out a radio, the MREs, and a few other sundry odds and ends I could do without to the other guys for their time. He and his friends shouted and waved as they turned around and drove back home under the steely gaze of the "Hawks."

Watching them go, I felt like a complete jackass for thinking for even one second that Jasim Madlool was anything but a good man.

My gear and I were loaded into one of the Humvees, and we started back the way I came. After a few hours, as it was already late in the day, Maj. Ward decided to make camp. I spent the chilly night on top of the major's vehicle, listening to one of the soldiers play his guitar magnificently as the others passed around my Thuraya sat phone to talk to their loved ones back in the States. Sorry about the phone bill, ABC.

Two days later, I hitched a ride to Kuwait City on an Air National Guard C-130. It took half a day to explain toto various Kuwaiti bureaucrats why my passport was missing an entry stamp, but I was eventually allowed onto a commercial jet to Dubai, and then the long flight home to Katie.

I sincerely hope Jasim survived the war and is living a long and happy life. And got the Nissan running again.

CHAPTER 45

THE ARMY OF THE FUTURE

In the winter of 2003, the Pentagon introduced a revolutionary new vehicle, the Stryker, as part of the vision Army chief of staff general Eric Shinseki had to transform the traditionally armor-heavy, slow-moving, massive entity into a more mobile, facile, and lethal fighting force. Shinseki's ideas were controversial and not always embraced by the military community, so the pressure was on him to prove his theories were correct. Thus, the Army threw the Third Brigade, Second Infantry Division into a trial by fire, deploying the ten-thousand-member unit, including its brand-new Stryker vehicles, to the hot bed of insurgency in Iraq, the restive city of Samarra. Somehow, a *Nightline* producer, Mike Gudgell, and I got permission to ride along with them as embedded journalists as they fought in and around the city.

Lt. Col. Buck James, with name, size, chiseled-jaw looks, and blunt manner, was a commander straight out of a Hollywood pitch meeting. "Samarra has been a thorn in the side as far back as recorded history," he told me. James had spent the past eighteen years as a paratrooper for the 82nd, then the 101st, then an Army Ranger. He saw his job in crystal-clear terms: clean up the city where most of its inhabitants still idolized Saddam Hussein. "It was always kind of Dodge City, kind of the Wild Wild West. A lot of criminal elements are there, a lot of arms dealers, and, I use the term loosely, but they're thugs. My mission is to find, kill, and capture these troublemakers."

At that point, over a thousand American soldiers and Marines had been killed in the war. Samarra and Fallujah were considered the two most dangerous places on earth for the American military.

This is the "Reporter's Notebook" piece I wrote for ABC's website:

> ABC News producer Mike Gudgell and I were walking along a dirt road at Camp Udari, Kuwait, just days before we headed into Iraq, when something large and lethal passed us from behind. A 20-ton, eight-wheeled, lightly armored Stryker.
>
> We never heard it coming.
>
> That was my first introduction to just how unique these armored personnel carriers really are, and why the Army has brought almost three hundred of the new vehicles to Iraq.
>
> They are spookily quiet. They are ridiculously fast. And they have coffee makers inside. The latter being the most salient point, according to the men who ride in these things. But the Army considers the first two qualities tactically crucial as they face off with a new type of enemy in a new kind of war. The insurgents setting off improvised explosive devices or firing rocket-propelled grenades at U.S. soldiers tend to not stand and fight a pitched battle. Rather they hit quickly and move away, sometimes not even staying around long enough to gauge the results of their attacks.
>
> So the soldiers of the 3rd Brigade of the 2nd Infantry Division, now known as the Stryker

Brigade, have adopted a new method of reacting to attacks: they rush towards the source, and they open the back hatch of the vehicles. Depending on how many vehicles are on patrol, out pours upwards of thirty highly trained infantrymen to chase down the insurgents. Meanwhile, the Strykers stay on the periphery, scanning the fields or buildings with their thermal cameras and covering the troops with a .50 caliber machinegun or Mk 19 automatic grenade launcher.

The tactic is new. The vehicles are new. The brigade is new.

It's all part of the transformation of the Army into what they hope will be a relevant force with units able to dash to trouble spots anywhere in the world, within 92 hours, and have with them enough fire-power to handle things. Right now, the Army is comprised of heavy mechanized divisions like the 3rd ID, which pummeled its way to Baghdad in historic fashion; or light divisions like the 101st Airborne, which has no armored vehicles, save a few "up-armored" Humvees, and very little heavy weaponry. There's nothing in the middle.

At least, not until now.

The 3rd Brigade, 2nd ID is the first of six such Stryker Brigades already funded and being constructed now, which comprise a true medium-weight force, meaning they're theoretically "light" enough to be flown hundreds of miles, but they're equipped with armor and, eventually, some big guns. Each Brigade is designed as an expeditionary force; that is, they can be sent to the corners of the world and function, and fight, independent of any support for up to three days. They have their own organic artillery units, intelligence units, and sniper units, with more snipers than most Army divisions have. The brigades are also issued their own UAVs, or Unmanned Aerial Vehicles—drone aircraft used to view a battlefield and send back real-time video so the unit's commanders have a clear idea of what lies before them.

Central to the unit's ability to "See first, act first, act decisively" is a computer system dubbed the FBCB2. There's a screen and keyboard next to the vehicle commander's seat. It links all the vehicles with each other and the entire command structure, so that a general at division headquarters can see on his 40-inch plasma screen a map showing exactly where every single Stryker is and where every enemy contact is. It's like the observer-mode in a video game, where you can watch it all unfold before you in real time. Each vehicle also has instant email ability, so the squad leader, for instance, can fire off a request for air support or medical evacuation.

As anyone not living in a cabin in the woods knows, with all this technology things are bound to go wrong. And they do. I've witnessed half-a-dozen Stryker computers crash or seize up. The radio communications, always the bane of the soldier in the field, still has problems. But this time, the Army put multiple radio systems in each vehicle, so that there's probably always at least one working. And the Army went one step further in keeping the units self-reliant as possible: each vehicle has a trained computer whiz on board, a soldier who can troubleshoot the problems—when he's not actually shooting at trouble, that is. Every soldier has more than one skill; auto-mechanic, medic, cook.

Most of the officers say that's what really makes this brigade unique: the quality of and training the soldiers receive. They have unprecedented responsibilities, and the field officers and sergeants are empowered to make command decisions quickly without having to run everything up the chain of command. The officers say that can mean the difference between catching a terrorist in the act, or just finding the bomb he was constructing.

And I keep reminding myself that this is, in effect, a shake-down cruise, albeit with life or death implications. The Stryker vehicles went from concept to combat in three years—nothing short of miraculous in a military that prefers to test, retest, and test again every system. It normally takes a minimum of eight years for new equipment to make it into the hands of soldiers.

The Strykers aren't perfect: it was discovered that their armor, even when bolstered with additional ceramic tiles, won't withstand certain kinds of rocket propelled grenades. So the Army quickly ordered "slat-armor" be installed, which theoretically catches rpg's and causes them to detonate inches away from the vehicle's skin. Some of the soldiers derisively call the addition "bird cages." But, as one battalion commander put it, "If it saves one guy's life, it's worth every penny."

The Strykers are heavier than expected now, with the additional armor, and wider. That means they probably can't be airlifted as far, as fast, as the Army projected. A rash of recent reports by the GAO and the Rand Corporation list other faults, and the main punch of the brigade, a Stryker-mounted 105 mm gun, is still years away from being fielded, if ever.

But since most of the soldiers in Iraq are being killed riding around in unprotected Humvees or trucks, the complaints of the critics fall on deaf ears with the guys who come and go from their foot-patrols in armored comfort.

Last night, less than a week after the unit arrived here in the so-called Sunni Triangle, the new equipment and tactics paid off for the first time. Alpha Company spotted two men in a field doing something suspicious. On their rubber tires, the huge vehicles slipped up close and the soldiers quickly captured the men, who had with them dynamite, mortar rounds, and AK-47 rifles. They were allegedly building another IED, or Improvised Explosive Device, the sort of boo-by-trap contraption that has killed and injured dozens of U.S. troops over the past months.

This is perhaps the most dangerous place in the world for Americans. Yet, almost five-thousand young men and women from Ft. Lewis, Washington have arrived here to relieve the weary and deserving troops who've dodged the frequent mortar attacks, rpg's and the baleful glares of the populace for seven or eight months now. When I rode into Iraq with the 101st Airborne during the opening stages of the war, we were greeted by cheering throngs of Iraqis. But that was south of Baghdad. Up here, you're more likely to get a thumb's down gesture than a wave. The people in this area had a benefactor in Saddam, and it's apparent, on the surface at least, that they deeply resent the Army's presence.

The Stryker Brigade's work in Iraq has only just begun. There are operations in the works that will tax the new equipment, the new technologies and certainly the new, and mostly very young, soldiers. It has already cost three young men their lives, when a Stryker slid sideways down one of the ubiquitous canals in this area and turned over. The three soldiers drowned. There will, we all fear, be more young people not going home.

That is the part of war that is never new. And so far, no technology yet invented can prevent it.

CHAPTER 46

GASTRONOMY

The most unusual things I've eaten in other countries:

Goat's eye soup, Morocco. Squishy.
Roasted lamb's ear, Kyrgyzstan. Leathery.
Durian fruit, Philippines. Stinky.
Fermented mare's milk (kumis), Central Asia. Sour.
Fermented cow's blood (in a Massai ceremony), Kenya. An honor.
Toasted grasshoppers, Burkina Faso. Crunchy.
Raw sea urchin, Grenada. Delicious.
Snake soup, Hong Kong. Tastes like chicken.
Tuna fish pizza, Taipei. Revolting.

CHAPTER 47

ON BEING GRONKED

Since the first scribe chiseled the news of an attack by saber tooth tigers on his neighbors onto the wall of a cave somewhere in France, journalists have always needed a thick skin, because there's always someone who objects to their reporting and expresses that displeasure in sometimes obscenely descriptive ways. But in the era of social media, the assaults and abuse and, frankly, craziness exploded. One might get used to the comments and voicemails and emails and direct messages, but after the first thousand or so it gets tiring.

I think I speak for all news reporters and producers when I say we welcome input from uninformed and aggressive members of the viewing public. It makes our day to read all-caps messages riddled with typos and misspellings, criticizing us for talking about things they don't want to hear about—like the dishonest politicians they worship, the climate change they've been brainwashed by certain media outlets into scoffing at, how a majority of Americans favor reproductive rights for women, or how the uneducated and underemployed in this nation somehow always find a way to vote against their own best interests. To this day I still enjoy the way so many outraged people refuse to discriminate between *their, there,* and *they're.* They all sound the same, so they must be interchangeable, I guess. And don't get me started on the elegant use of incorrect personal pronouns. Myself believes the education system in this nation is second to none.

Once upon a time, all we had to contend with was the occasional review by a handful of newspaper media critics. That specialty has pretty much gone the way of the dodo—very few newspapers now devote column inches to discussing television news. Perhaps the millions of red-faced, spittle-launching experts on Facebook and Instagram and various websites made those jobs obsolete.

Nevertheless, getting the attention of media gossip columnists could sometimes be a good thing, or at least ego fulfilling. In 2008, I got a call from my agent, whose wife was thumbing through the *National Enquirer* at the grocery checkout stand and was surprised to spot a photograph inside of yours truly. This was the much anticipated/dreaded annual *55 Best and Worst Beach Bodies* issue. I was desperately hoping I wasn't being featured in that particular article.

I wandered over to the local drugstore and picked up a copy, furtively scanning the shoppers to my left and right to make sure no one noticed what I was reading. All of a sudden I was eight years old again, sneaking a peek at the Holy Grail of porn, *Hustler* magazine, my dad kept hidden under the mattress.

At the bottom of page two was the headline "Couric Replacement Ready to Step In," along with photos of me and Katie Couric, who was the CBS News main anchor at the time. The byline was a reporter by the name of Jeff Samuels.

Couric's brief tenure at the Tiffany Network had been, in a word, rough. After two years at the desk her ratings were in the tank, and the staff wasn't exactly in love with America's Sweetheart, who, behind closed doors, could be anything but. I've known at least two female anchors who were undercut by her machinations when she felt threatened by them. I also had a personal experience with her duplicity while covering the massacre at Columbine High School in Colorado, when every news outlet agreed to go through a single intercessor for interview requests to the family members to prevent them from being overwhelmed at such a tragic time, and Couric bypassed the agreement to personally pitch an exclusive for the *Today* show.

I had left ABC News shortly prior to this for an anchor job at CBS's New York flagship station. When David Friend, the news director there at the time, called me out of the blue to offer me the job, I'd just finished up yet another long stretch of war coverage. My friend and colleague Bob Woodruff had just been terribly wounded by an IED in Iraq, and our kids were of similar ages, so I was feeling that maybe I'd pushed my luck long enough. Not being shot at or blown up while also being home on weekends seemed like a terrific career and personal move. But, to be clear, there was absolutely no discussion of my joining the network during those negotiations.

The *Enquirer* article starts out, "Katie Couric's bosses at CBS have found her replacement on the 'Evening News'— and Katie is breathing a sigh of relief. After suffering through two years of dismal ratings and scorching criticism, sources say the 51-year old former 'Today' show host is quietly hoping for a new and more fulfilling assignment at the network. She may get her wish, as CBS is considering handing her job to rising star Don Dahler after the presidential election in November." Samuels said CBS denied she was leaving the broadcast and that I would be her replacement, but he then quoted an unnamed CBS insider: "Don is exactly what CBS is looking for—young, smart, and with no baggage. He'd make an ideal anchor and can grow into the job."

It simply wasn't true. I don't know if my name ever did come up in high-level discussions at the network, but even if so, they never went beyond that. Neither my agent nor I ever heard a peep about it from the folks upstairs. That's the problem with gossip and, now, social media. So much of it is completely made up, or exaggerated for reasons of someone's agenda, or simply mean-spirited.

Case in point to the latter: an article years earlier in the *New York Post* by Michele Greppi, its longtime media critic who called herself "tvgirrrl" (despite being middle-aged). The headline read, "ABC'S AMATEUR HOUR: DON DAHLER AND HOW NOT TO HOST 'GMA.'"

Ouch.

It was my first time filling in for Charlie Gibson. Shelley Ross, *Good Morning America*'s executive producer, paired me up with a fellow child of the military, Elizabeth Vargas, for the Memorial Day broadcast. Shelley asked us to chat about life in the military whenever it was appropriate and decided she wanted me to dress casually.

Tvgrrrl didn't appreciate either. "He and Elizabeth Vargas (subbing for Diane Sawyer) made local morning anchors seem like 'MacNeil/Lehrer' clones. It was 'Amateur Hour' times two. And we don't mean just the segments in which Dahler and Vargas compared military upbringings illustrated with maps showing where each had lived, as if we care." Then she upped the nastiness factor. "Dahler, whose look became more Details-oriented after he got hot and heavy with ex-CBS Newsie, ex-NBC Newsie and ex-'Access Hollywood' starlet Giselle Fernandez, couldn't even be bothered to wear a tie on 'GMA' Monday. He may or may not have bothered to wear a collar. We couldn't tell."

Ah, there's the rub. Tvgrrrl really, *really* hated my girlfriend. I have no idea why, but she used her column to excoriate Giselle on a regular basis. So this article was another chance to take a swipe at her, finishing it with the snarky line: "If Dahler's smart, he'll start his own page on Fernandez's vanity website and jump when the first window in his 'GMA' contract opens. Otherwise, odds are that he'll be pushed."

By the way, I ran into Greppi at a charity function years later. She had the good grace to bring up that particular column and apologize.

My point is that everyone has a right to their opinion, and even though it can be embarrassing or even painful to be on the receiving end of those opinions, a television journalist has to either accept it as part of the job or get out of the business. I completely accept the possibility that I did suck that morning as a fill-in for Charlie Gibson. But the internet has made things a million times worse. Now, not only can a handful of critics or viewers who write nasty letters, care of your station or network, take a shot at you, but the World Wide Web has empowered hordes of angry, clueless, vindictive cowards who instantly fire off the vilest comments and insults if they don't like a particular report, or hairdo, or outfit, without any repercussions—such as a punch in the nose. Which is what many of these nutjobs would receive if they said some of things they do in person.

Like the time I got "Gronked."

A little background here: as most football fans know, Rob Gronkowski was arguably the greatest tight end who ever played in the NFL. During his years with the New England Patriots, the six-foot-six, 265-pound beast, coupled with the GOAT, Tom Brady, tore through defenses on the way to multiple Super Bowl wins.

In 2010 the Patriots added to its powerhouse offense by drafting another standout tight end, Aaron Josef Hernandez. He ran the forty-yard dash in 4.64 seconds and could bench-press 225 pounds thirty times in a row. Team owner Robert Kraft was aware Hernandez had a troubled past, but he later said he believed the team's culture, and coach Bill Belichick, could straighten him out. The duo of Gronkowski and Hernandez proved almost unstoppable. Hernandez was eventually signed to a five-year deal worth $39.58 million. But his troubles continued.

On June 18, 2013, the police showed up at Hernandez's home with a search warrant. A man named Odin Lloyd, a friend of his, had been found shot to death in an industrial park a mile away. Eight days later, Hernandez was charged with first-degree murder.

A month after he was jailed, I found myself in the Gronkowski family home, surrounded by Rob, his brothers (all phenomenal athletes)—Chris, Dan, Gordie Jr., and Glenn (Goose)—and their parents, Gordy and Diane. We were there to tape a story for *GMA* about Gordy's new book, *Growing Up Gronk*. As the camera crew set up lights, Diane served sandwiches and soft drinks, and the brothers played a raucous game of indoor basketball in the living room. Looking on, I chatted with the elder Gronkowski about his sons, how he and his wife raised them to be respectful but determined, and Aaron Hernandez.

Gordy talked about how painful it was for Rob. How he probably knew Hernandez best given how much time they spent together at practices and team events, even though his teammate wasn't exactly the most outgoing person.

The entire family, except Diane, positioned themselves on a large couch for the interview. When the cameras rolled, I asked them about the book, their training as athletes, and how it was growing up in a family of such high achievers. It was a funny, light, comfortable discussion. At one point, Gordy grew emotional talking about when any of his boys would get injured. It was a beautifully authentic moment that any parent could relate to.

Then, because I'm a reporter and it's my job, I asked Rob about Hernandez. I'm certain he knew it was coming. And he had a response already loaded in the chamber.

"I do have to ask you, when you heard about Aaron Hernandez, what you thought, what your reaction was?"

He was no longer smiling that famous Gronk grin, "Ahhhh, next question." His brothers chuckled. "I learned that from Drew Rosenhaus [Rob's agent]. Next question."

I tried again, because that's what journalism (and football, by the way) is—not giving up when you meet that first obstacle. "It had to be a shock to you; it had to be a shock for all your teammates."

"Next question." Even more laughter. Louder. The wide shot of the interview shows everyone in the room having a good chuckle. They knew their brother wasn't really mad.

I turned to their father. "Alright, then I'll ask you. It seems to me that these two men played on opposite sides of the line, but they are more than that in terms of being opposites." Keep in mind—this was exactly what we had just been discussing off camera.

"Truthfully, I'm not going to go there," Gordy said. I completely understood that reaction, and I intended to let it go. But since he was so compelling during our earlier talk, I had wanted to give him the opportunity to share his thoughts with the world.

That's when Rob waved his hand and stood up. "I'm outta here." Even more laughter. He feigned taking off his microphone.

"Don't walk off," I said, also laughing. "I'll change the subject."

Gronk immediately sat back down, and we continued the interview. When it finally ended, Gordy and the brothers, including Rob, all signed a copy of the book for me and shook my hand or gave me a hug, and we parted on great terms. That was it. That was all the drama there was.

But not according to dozens of sports websites, social media pages, and thousands of online commentators whose passions about their football heroes eclipsed their grasp of journalism and, frankly, logic. I've been called "sleazy," "slimy reporter," "skeezball," and "shitty." OK. As I said before, everyone is entitled to their opinions. Words will never hurt as much as a pop in the nose. But here's the thing—some commentators, even some sports reporters, accused me of breaking an agreement to not bring up the allegations of murder. One idiot went so far as to insist he knew for certain that was a condition of the interview to begin with.

Uh, no. Not only is that against my own professional ethics, but it's strictly in violation of ABC News policy. We don't hand out questions beforehand, and we don't agree to not ask about anything. The subject can say, as Gronk did, "no comment," but any real journalist would never agree to any restriction on what can and cannot be asked.

I was accused, in effect, of bullying him by asking about Hernandez twice. Really? A professional football player who happens to be six inches taller and three times as muscular was intimidated by little ole me? The guy runs over people for a living. He's got more personality than half of Florida. But it was unfair for this reporter to press him a little on the biggest story of the day? Poor Gronk. Good thing he has so many anonymous "experts" to back him up. "Ask and move on," advised one genius on Reddit. So, I guess he thinks that when Gronk hit the line and didn't get through the first try, he should just sit down too.

I never used to spend much time worrying about what these kinds of misinformed, ignorant people think. But not long ago a conversation with my teenage son opened my eyes to how long-lasting such comments truly are. He asked me how I could stand being so hated. I wasn't sure what he meant until he showed me one of the sports websites he spends a lot of time on that had resurrected the Gronkowski clip, spawning hundreds more vicious comments. I tried to explain what being a reporter means, and that Gronk was actually just joking around. But I'm not sure he believed me.

Because if someone says it on the internet it must be true. Right?

CHAPTER 48

THE DAY THE EARTH MOVED

I was *this close* to being done for the day. The alarm had gone off at 2:00 a.m. so that I could get up, shower, dress, and arrive at the WCBS studios in time to fill in as anchor of the morning and noon shows, a shift that begins at 4:30 a.m. and normally wrapped up by 12:30 p.m., but I had a story to finish writing for air another day so was hanging around a bit longer.

It was August 23, 2011. 1:51 p.m. My sleepy ass was planning to be headed out the front door on West Fifty-Seventh Street at two sharp. Nine more minutes. I had visions of a nice nap.

Then the earth moved. Literally.

A magnitude 5.8 earthquake slammed the Piedmont region of Virginia and was felt across a dozen states, including New York. Including Manhattan. Including the CBS Broadcast Center on West Fifty-Seventh Street. In fact, that particular temblor was felt by more people than any other in US history.

The newsroom began shaking. Everyone looked at each other, wondering if perhaps it was an explosion. Ten years after 9/11 and our minds still immediately went to *terror attack*. That's when the news director, David Friend, came running out of his office and shouted, "It's an earthquake!"

He scanned the room, his gaze settling on me. "Dahler! Get on the air! Now!"

The main news studio was dark, having shut down after the noon broadcast. All the camera operators and technicians had yet to be replaced by their evening counterparts. The only option was the remote-controlled camera that sat in one corner of the newsroom, used primarily for updates during the day or live shots by reporters during broadcasts.

I wiggled the IFB back into my ear so that the director could talk to me from the control room and settled onto the barstool in front of the camera. Barely a minute later and the *Special Report* graphics appeared on the TV monitor next to the camera. Suddenly I was live.

The teleprompter on the front of the camera lens was blank. No script. No information. Nothing but whatever I could find between my ears to tell a few million scared viewers. Imagine yourself in that situation. Something has just happened, and you don't know most of the details, but three… two…one…you're on the air. Go.

A really talented news writer, Ambrose Raftery, leaned over and handed me a statement from the United States Geological Survey with the longitude and latitude of the epicenter just as I was telling whoever was watching that they did, in fact, feel what they thought they felt. Reporters and live trucks were being dispatched around the city. Producers were manning the phones, trying to get details. And my mug was on television sets all over the East Coast.

So, here's why I always tell students at schools where I'm asked to speak that the most important thing a journalist can do is *read*. Read everything. Read history, and science, and biographies. Read magazines. Read books. Read all the time. Be curious. It's a career of constant learning. Because you never know when some little bit of information, stuck against some crevice of your skull, is going to come in handy. We won't always have Google at our fingertips.

It just so happens I'd just read a long magazine article about earthquakes a week earlier, and enough of that material was still bouncing around in my brain for me to speak somewhat knowledgably about what was going on.

For the next one and a half hours, I ad-libbed about the three types of faults—normal, reverse, strike-slip—and where the known fault lines lay on the Eastern Seaboard. I warned viewers to get away from their homes and into an open area in case of aftershocks. When reporters began calling in on phones or their microwave trucks were up and running, I talked to them about what they were seeing and hearing. I interviewed callers who phoned in from around the area. As time passed, producers and writers would slip me pieces of paper with more information from the government, or tidbits about past quakes, or anecdotes from other people on the East Coast who were going through the same thing.

One and a half hours of unscripted talk about an experience we were all sharing felt as though it flew by.

When the evening anchors eventually came in and the studio was fired up, I signed off. As I unclipped my mic and stepped away from the barstool, the entire newsroom stood and applauded.

CHAPTER 49

THAT WEEK IN APRIL

Four hours, nine minutes, and forty-three seconds into the race, a loud explosion was heard, followed by another just seconds later. Two hundred miles away, in the CBS's Manhattan newsroom, I was standing next to the assignment desk chatting with a writer about my story for the night when someone said loudly, "Something's going on at the Boston Marathon!"

"It may have been a manhole explosion," said a desk assistant. "But I'm seeing early reports of injuries."

Without hesitation, an *Evening News* senior producer, Guy Campanile (who's now with *60 Minutes*), pointed to me and a talented young producer named Arden Farhi and said, "Get on a plane. Now."

We both ran to our offices, grabbed our go bags (which were always packed and ready) and hailed a cab out front of the West Fifty-Seventh Street studios. Normally the trip across town to LaGuardia Airport can take an hour and a half or more. This day, for whatever reason, the New York traffic parted for us as if Moses were our driver, and we dashed through ticketing and security and onto what ended up being the last plane allowed into Boston for days to come in less than forty minutes. Police blocked our cab from getting any closer to the scene than Storrow Drive, so Arden and I threw our bags over our shoulders and hoofed it all the way to

Massachusetts General Hospital. Thus began days of nonstop, around-the-clock reporting.

Two terrorists, brothers Dzhokhar and Tamerlan Tsarnaev, had planted homemade pressure cooker bombs among the bystanders at the Boston Marathon. The subsequent explosions killed three people, maimed seventeen, and injured hundreds of others. When our flight landed and we made our way into the city, the police still didn't have any idea who the suspects were. Arden and I filed our first live report from one of the hospitals tasked with caring for the many victims. Boston officials quickly shut down all traffic into and out of the city.

In the days that followed, we interviewed some of those victims, including a dancer, Adrianne Haslet-Davis, and newlyweds Patrick Downes and Jessica Kensky, who were all grievously, permanently injured. We spoke regularly to Boston's police commissioner, Ed Davis, for updates on the investigation. Within three days, by laboriously scouring dozens of photos, videos, and security camera footage, detectives were able to narrow down their search to two men seen placing small backpacks on the ground and suspiciously walking away. The police released still images of the two, and within hours they had their names. The date was April 18.

That evening, while we were enjoying a sushi dinner, investigative producer Len Tepper got a tip that police suspected there was a connection between the brothers and the Massachusetts Institute of Technology. Something about a ball cap one of the suspects had been photographed wearing. Len also had the name of a specific dorm that might be of interest. So Arden and I, along with producers Jamie McGlinchy and Sally Rosen, hopped in a rental car and drove out to the university to see if we could spot any police cars or nondescript federal vehicles staking out any of the buildings. As we drove slowly through the quiet streets, we saw nothing out of the ordinary and eventually returned to our hotel.

About an hour later, around midnight, Arden got a call from CBS's *National Desk* about unconfirmed police activity at MIT. I had just fallen asleep when my cell rang. "Something's up at MIT," Arden said. "Let's go." The two of us met downstairs a few minutes later and drove back out to the university.

It was later revealed in court that at 10:35 p.m. the Tsarnaev brothers shot and killed an MIT policeman, Sean Collier, and carjacked a Chinese immigrant by the name of Dun Meng. Meng eventually managed to escape and run into a gas station, where the attendant phoned the police. That's when the dragnet began to tighten. Dzhokhar and Tamerlan were confronted by officers at 12:45 a.m., and a shootout ensued that saw the brothers throwing more homemade bombs. The older Tsarnaev suffered multiple gunshot wounds and was run over by Dzhokhar while trying to escape. He died in the hospital, but his younger brother got away.

We made it back to MIT as thousands of cops were descending on the area. A perimeter was established, and we were ordered back behind it. Then it was moved back even farther to the Target parking lot. Producers Jamie McGlinchy and Chris St. Peter joined us, as did cameraman David Gladstone and truck operator Mike Meinhardt. Armored vehicles with officers in tactical gear roared past us. They were conducting a house-to-house search in Watertown for Dzhokhar, who was still armed and dangerous but believed to be injured.

We first went live at the scene at around 2:00 a.m. and kept reporting on and off through the following morning, day, and into the evening. With a constant stream of information supplied by police and FBI contacts developed by us, Len Tepper, and CBS News's other brilliant investigative producer, Pat Milton, I was able to feed our viewers instant updates, sometimes with exclusive information. There were times while I was on air when one of the finest journalists to ever sit in an anchor chair, Scott Pelley, grilled me as to whether I had confirmation of this fact or other, and I could always assure him I had at least two sources every time. The network was in special report mode the entire day, with us taking point.

At 6:00 p.m., a resident of Watertown spotted the terrorist hiding in a boat in his backyard and notified police. We got early word of that development, even as we saw helicopters shift over to Tsarnaev's location. Police were able to use thermal cameras to see the murderer lying in the bottom of the boat. At some point, they shot him, and he climbed out of the boat to surrender.

Just as network programming commitments were about to take our special report off the air, a cheer went up from all the law enforcement officers around our live shot location. "We got him!" one of the cops shouted at me. A caravan of armored vehicles sped past us, with Dzhokhar Tsarnaev inside one of them. The camera panned as it passed our position, and Scott signed off a few minutes later. The timing was remarkable. It couldn't have been scripted better.

The trial began on March 4, not quite a year after the bombings occurred, involving more than 90 witnesses. I covered almost every minute of the proceedings. The jury endured heart-wrenching testimony and saw horrific images and videos before handing down guilty verdicts on all 30 counts on April 8.

Tsarnaev was ultimately sentenced to death.

CHAPTER 50

CODA

The call came on a May morning in 2020, just a few months after the pandemic began. It was from the president of CBS News, Susan Zirinsky, and the head of talent for the network, Laurie Orlando. You know when two executives are double-teaming you that the news probably isn't good.

Actually, to be completely honest, I was expecting it. The network was hemorrhaging money trying to cover this thing no one yet fully understood. Revenues were down; expenses were way up. That's the traditional formula for corporate layoffs. And I, a journeyman correspondent getting a little long in the tooth and pulling one of the higher salaries for nonanchors, had a gigantic bull's-eye on my back in the shape of a dollar sign.

Z, as everyone affectionately calls her, was sincerely upset. We've known each other a long time, even before I joined CBS. There are two reasons why she's so loved and respected: she truly, deeply cares for her people, and she truly, deeply cares for journalism. Laurie, on the other hand, was less sentimental, although gracious. It was her job to infuse the news division with younger, more diverse talent, and I'm sure she saw my departure as an opportunity to build the bench. I hold no animosity toward her at all. I tried to assure them both that it was OK and that I understood. It would be, in effect, an early retirement, with a generous severance package including health care coverage for a year.

In reality, the timing couldn't have been better. Only days earlier I landed a new book contract with a respected publishing house to write the definitive biography of the first licensed female pilot in America, Harriet Quimby, whose story was lost to history because of a terrible tragedy. I'd published three novels over the past decade, to varying degrees of success, but I was both excited and intimidated by the prospect of researching and writing a nonfiction book. Having the time now to do so was a blessing. I sent the following email to my friends and colleagues at CBS:

> Subject: So Long, and Thanks for All the Fish
>
> Let me say this right at the top: given the life-and-death struggle we as a species are going through right now; the loved ones we've lost and stand to lose, and the financial heartbreak, fear, and realities faced by millions, the fact that I am now counted among the unemployed, after many, many decades in this fantastic business, is an insignificant development.
>
> No really. I mean that. I'm going to be fine. We're going to be fine. Don't feel bad for me. We're all healthy here in the wilds of Jersey, and ultimately that's the main thing that matters.
>
> So don't feel bad, except, perhaps, because I will no longer get to see you all in the mornings, or hear your ideas on the calls, or visit you in the other bureaus, or haggle with a brilliant producer over an additional [00]:10 or turn of phrase on a script, or hover over an artist in the edit room debating a change of one particular shot, or scramble onto

an airplane and then haul ass to a breaking news story, or experience the thrill of winging it on a live shot, or, frankly, do what I was born to do, what I always wanted to do, and that is report for the best news operation in the world. You can feel bad about that. Because I do. I will miss all that and you terribly.

I suspect you'll be seeing a lot of goodbye messages over the coming days and weeks, so I'll keep mine brief:

It's been an honor.

They did see more goodbye messages in the ensuing weeks and months, a lot more. As I learned so painfully twenty years earlier when I got the same call from ABC News just prior to 9/11, broadcast journalism isn't just a public service anymore; it's also a business, one that is expected to make money for the corporations that own the news operations. It wasn't always that way, but when politicians gutted the FCC during the Reagan era, reporting the news devolved from trying to understand the world and convey that understanding accurately to the American public—while being held accountable—to trying to find as many eyeballs as possible, and thus advertising dollars, by appealing to the lowest public interests and political biases. Truth was the first casualty of that tectonic change, and that gave rise to the various news sites and cable networks bent on appealing to their "constituents" without regulation, without integrity, without any commitment to actually serving the public good. Americans have become less educated, less informed, less engaged in the world, and more angry about the cynical distortions being fed them by the likes of Fox News: the Dunning-Kruger effect writ large.

The call from Z changed my life in very dramatic ways, but in some very good ways as well. For the first time since

Jack and Callie were born, we all had dinners together, almost every night. I was around enough now to help Katie shoulder the burdens of day-to-day family life, which she had somehow managed to do despite a very important and demanding career of her own. I closed down the little farm we were selling and found great homes for the horses, goats, and chickens. I said goodbye to the life that had given me so many unforgettable moments through the years and began writing the newest chapter, as clichéd as that sounds.

Yes, I still miss answering the trumpet call when there's breaking news, dashing out into the field with a team of professionals at the top of their game. I miss the adrenaline rush of doing interviews, getting images, writing a script, and going live at the scene under deadline, and doing it right and doing it well. I miss getting to duck under the velvet rope and have access to places and people we rarely get to experience. I miss crafting visual, compelling stories that lead viewers to feel something, to experience some part of the human existence they would not ordinarily be privy to, to learn something they didn't know. But I had my time. It's someone else's turn.

As I read back through these last few paragraphs, it occurs to me that, were I a young person dreaming of a life of adventure and learning, I'd be thinking: well, that's all fine and good for you, but how the hell do I get there? I benefited from so many ridiculously fortunate twists along my journey that are impossible to replicate. It also helped that I was a white male. Despite the early struggles of my life, I am clearly aware of that specific and unfair cultural advantage. I hope I'm not wrong to believe things are finally getting better in that regard.

So, in the form of a warning, I'll first quote Socrates: "I know that I know nothing." Take what I'm about to say with a grain of salt. Because if there's one thing I'm absolutely certain about, it's that everyone has to chart his or her own path. There's no secret to any of this.

But, that said, here goes:

1. Never make a career choice based solely on money.
2. Read. Everything. Knowledge isn't just power; it's jet fuel.
3. Be curious. Be nosy. And, at times, be a pain in the ass.
4. Cultivate friends along the way and help them whenever you can.
5. Technology is today's paper and pen. Learn how to use it all.
6. Don't be afraid to dream big, but just know it will always take work.
7. When the bosses are wrong, tell them. They're only human.
8. And, finally, eat the goat's eye soup. Sleep on the ground. Face your fears.

Do things you'd never imagine. And mostly, walk among people who are different from you and listen to their stories, without holding a mirror to your own face. It's never about you. It's always about them. Move well.

Best of luck. I'll be watching.

ABOUT THE AUTHOR

Don Dahler has been a fixture on national network news for over three decades. During his career, he received every major award for broadcast journalism, including a Peabody, a duPont-Columbia Award, two Emmys, two Edward R. Murrow Awards, and a New York Press Club journalism award. He also covered major news stories, such as global wars, school shootings, presidential elections, and natural disasters. He was the first network correspondent to report live from the scene on 9/11. A summa cum laude graduate of the University of North Carolina at Charlotte, his career as a journalist, filmmaker, novelist, and biographer led him to over 120 countries, often living in places like Africa and Asia for months at a time. He was born in Colorado Springs to an Air Force family and now resides in New Jersey with his wife, two children, two dogs, two cats, and a gecko. He is an avid golf, tennis, and pickleball player.